A Deadly Modeling Job : The True Story of Elodie Morel

Ruth Kanton

Published by Trellis Publishing, 2021.

While every precaution has been taken in the preparation of this book, the publisher assumes no responsibility for errors or omissions, or for damages resulting from the use of the information contained herein.

A DEADLY MODELING JOB : THE TRUE STORY OF ELODIE MOREL

First edition. July 1, 2021.

Copyright © 2021 Ruth Kanton.

ISBN: 979-8224291496

Written by Ruth Kanton.

A DEADLY MODELING JOB : THE TRUE STORY OF ELODIE MOREL

RUTH KANTON

On Monday, May 2, 2005, at 5:45 p.m., a call was received at the Aigues-Mortes police station in southern France. The caller, 63-year-old Dominique Tarasco, had a bizarre tale for police. He told the police that a crime was about to occur and that they needed to work fast to stop it. According to Tarasco, one of his friends was carrying a gun and was planning on abducting a girl. He said that the man was at his place of business when he announced his plans and left. However, despite the police's efforts to get the name of the man, Tarasco categorically refused to provide it. He told police that all he could tell them was that the man was heading to a bar at the port in Aigues-Mortes, and that he had a green-grey SEAT Ibiza parked in a particular parking lot near the bar.

Tarasco urged police to respond fast, stating that the couple was just about to arrive at the bar. The Aigues-Mortes police took the information seriously, and scrambled to get their resources in place. The first call was to the Nîmes public prosecutor. They were able to reach the deputy prosecutor instead, who quickly authorized a surveillance operation after he was apprised of the situation. Patrol officers were dispatched to the area near Bar de L' Escale to find and keep an eye of the SEAT Ibiza. Two officers sat by the terrace of the bar and pretended to be having a drink, while two other officers positioned themselves discreetly in the corners of the bar. However, police were already at a disadvantage because the information provided by Tarasco was not enough to identify either the man or his intended victim. To make matters worse, it had been a three day weekend, so the bar was filled with couples. Officers at the station tried to get Tarasco to provide at least descriptive information about the man, but he adamantly refused.

Officers had arrived at the scene at 6:15 p.m., and after an hour, they were no closer to identifying any suspicious couples. Patrol officers were still keeping an eye out for a grey-green SEAT Ibiza, but there was none in the area. Officers decided to make another call to Tarasco to try and get more information. He maintained that he was not giving the name of the man, and every effort officers made to get any more information was futile. Finally, one officer asked Tarasco whether he was sure the vehicle police should be looking for was a grey-green SEAT Ibiza. After a few moments, Tarasco told police that he had made a mistake regarding the description of the car. Instead, they should be looking for a grey Honda City ZX. When the information was passed on to the patrol officers, they stated that a ZX had actually passed them a few moments back, but they had not paid attention to the vehicle or its occupants since at the time their focus was on SEAT Ibizas. It seemed that their informant was giving them incomplete and false information. However, this was not enough for them to call off the surveillance just yet.

Dominique Tarasco

Despite his obvious false information and reluctance to provide more information to the police, officers still took Tarasco's urgent warning seriously. This is because he was a well-known figure in the community, and he often interacted with the criminals in the area. Tarasco was officially a scrap merchant, but he also ran a popular underground nightclub in the region, which was frequented by celebrities as well as less reputable individuals. The parties he threw in the club were legendary, and they allowed Tarasco to rub shoulders with crooks and gangsters, and he was able to pick up valuable information about crimes in the area. Tarasco freely shared some of this information with the police, and in exchange police protected his nightclub. As an informant, Tarasco's information had led to the arrest of various minor criminals including drug traffickers and car thieves.

After Tarasco changed the description of the car, police told him to carry on with his day and that they would keep investigating. He went for dinner in town, and spent some time drinking. At around 1 a.m., as he was driving home, Tarasco came upon a police roadblock. It was a routine traffic stop, but he believed that it was part of the investigation he had helped launched that evening. He parked his car and approached police, asking them about whether they were still searching for the grey ZX. The officers at the scene were unaware of what Tarasco was talking about, and as he tried explaining the situation, a grey ZX passed by the scene. He caught a glimpse of his friend in the driver's seat, with a woman in the passenger side. She was leaning against the window, and he assumed she was asleep. He began shouting at police to arrest the man and seize the vehicle, "That's him. Do something. Arrest him. Stop him now. That's the guy."

The police had no reason to make an arrest since the car had not entered the roadblock, and Tarasco watched as the vehicle drove off. A few moments later, his phone rang. It was the man in question. "Where are you?" the man asked, then went on to warn Tarasco about the roadblock by the fountain. "He's just called me. That's him," Tarasco shouted at the police. However, the officers chased him off the scene and told him that he was pissing them off. He got back into his car and drove home.

Potential Victim

On May 4, 2005, two days after Tarasco's call to the Aigues-Mortes police department, a 25-year-old man walked into the 2nd Arrondissement Police Station in Marseille. He looked worried and shaken up, and he demanded to talk to a police officer. When he was finally directed to an officer, he immediately stated that he wanted to report the disappearance of his wife, 29-year-old Elodie Morel. He stated that she was a waitress, and that he hadn't heard from her in about 48 hours. He explained that they had a little boy together, and that it was unusual that he hadn't heard from her. He told the officer that 15 days prior, Elodie had signed up to an online casting website. She had always dreamt of becoming a model, and with her modest income, she was hoping to earn more money.

As she browsed the available jobs on the site, she came across an advertisement by a woman looking for someone to represent the Rolls

Royce brand in a new publicity campaign. The ad promised an attractive compensation of €5,000 for a five-day shoot. Elodie sent a message to the advertiser, a photographer named Nicole Forestier. The two seemed to hit it off, and they exchange a couple of emails for a few days. She finally got a message informing her that she had been chosen as the face of the campaign, and that they needed to schedule a meeting in Aigues-Mortes. Elodie's husband told the officer that he had never seen his wife that excited about anything before. She seemed so happy, and she felt confident that it was not a scam because a woman was behind it. A meeting was scheduled at Bar de L 'Escale on May 2, 2005. She prepared for the meeting, making sure she could flawlessly apply her makeup, and packed her favorite clothes. She was worried about her son, since she had never been away from him for that long. She promised to check in with her husband, and on the morning of May 2, she left her home driving the couple's old BMW. He explained that she had sent him a message at 9:30 p.m. saying: "Big kiss. Everything is going well. I'll call you tomorrow when I can. Hugs and kisses. Talk later."

Since then, he explained, he had not heard from his wife again. He stated that he had called her a number of times, but that her phone had been switched off. He was convinced that something bad had happened, and he believed that maybe she had been trafficked for sex or was forced into a prostitution ring. He urged the officer to do something to find his wife. However, the officer was not entirely convinced that Elodie was missing. The husband had explained that they were having marital problems, and that this had been going on for the past few months. They were separating, and had already filed for divorce. When the officer tried explaining that his wife could have merely run away, he adamantly refused. He began causing a scene, and he was so belligerent that the officer agreed to launch a nationwide investigation.

The 2nd Arrondissement Police Station created wanted posters for Elodie Morel, and faxed the information to police departments all over France.

Investigation

When officers at the Aigues-Mortes police department received the fax, the details provided by the 2nd Arrondissement seemed to match up with their case. On May 2, the search had been called off sometime after 6 p.m. after they were unable to find a man acting threateningly towards a young woman. No additional information had been recovered from the surveillance, so the officers had just written a report. However, the information they had received seemed to correspond to Tarasco's information, particularly the dates and locations provided. The fax also provided the police with additional information including Elodie's name, address, phone number, the car she was driving, as well as her husband's name and phone number. They quickly called him, and he recounted the story he told the officer in Marseille. Police in Aigues-Mortes asked him to come down to their station as soon as he could, and immediately launched an official investigation into the disappearance of Elodie Morel.

They traced her phone, which showed that on the night of May 2, it had emitted a signal in Aigues-Mortes then Saint-Laurent-d'Aigouze then Saint Gilles before it stopped emitting signals after pinging in Ververt. Following this discovery, the Nîmes investigative team decided to take over the investigation from the Aigues-Mortes police. They set up base in Ververt Police Station and began their investigation. Every available unit in the region was mobilized to patrol the streets, country roads, and paths where Elodie's phone had been tracked to. Elodie's husband arrived at the Aigues-Mortes police station at around 2 a.m., and gave police more photos of his wife. He stated that Elodie was strong and combative, saying: "Elodie has certainly struggled. Therefore she understood that the meeting was nothing but a trap. Elodie is no fool. She always knew how to react in difficult situations."

He told the officers that maybe Elodie had fought the attacker and enraged him, leading to her murder. Meanwhile the patrols were proving futile since there was not much information to guide the search.

Investigators were getting frustrated, especially because they knew someone who could provide pertinent information about the case. On Thursday May 5, 2005, Dominique Tarasco was scheduled to appear at the station for a formal interview at 8:30 a.m. Investigators asked him to identify the man, since they had a potential victim they needed to find as soon as possible. Tarasco refused to give the name. The investigators pushed for hours, but he maintained that he was afraid of being killed by a psychopath. When the prosecutor was called in, he tried pleading with Tarasco to help them save the girl, but he adamantly refused. Frustrated, the prosecutor threatened to arrest him. Afraid of getting arrested and charged with a crime, Tarasco gave up a name a few moments later – Gillaume Mingaud.

Gillaume Mingaud

Tarasco told police that Mingaud was working as a security guard at his nightclub. He stated that Mingaud had been in prison on several occasions, and that everyone who knew him was afraid of him. He was prone to violence, and that anything could set him off. Additionally, Mingaud always had a weapon on him, mostly a knife, but he was known to carry a gun on occasion. When they check his arrest record, police discovered that Mingaud had been convicted of the rape of two 20-year-old German tourists. He picked them up when they were hitchhiking, and drove them to Camargue. He threatened them and then proceeded to rape them almost all through the night. He spent nine years in prison for the crime. He had also been sentenced several times for possession of arms, and was known for armed violence. With this information, investigators believed that the way forward was to use Tarasco to lure Mingaud into their custody.

Arrests

Under the watchful eye of investigators and the prosecutor, Tarasco arranged a meeting with Guillaume Mingaud. The two men agreed to meet in the parking lot of an old nightclub in Ververt at around 6 p.m. Police positioned themselves near the nightclub and waited for Mingaud to arrive. At 6 p.m., a van drove into the club's parking lot. Immediately the two occupants of the van alighted and entered the club, police apprehended them. Mingaud took off running, but he was tackled to the ground by one of the investigators and handcuffed. When police conducted a body search, they found Elodie's bank card in one of Mingaud's jean pockets. He immediately offered an explanation for it, stating that he had found it in a bar and that he had plans to return it to its owner.

Police turned their attention to Mingaud's companion, 55-year-old Richard Lignier. Richard was unknown to police, and seemed to have no criminal affiliations. He was just a local resident, and lived with his family. When asked what he was doing at the scene, he promptly replied that he just Mingaud's old friend. He told the investigators that whenever Mingaud was in the area, he would stay at his home. This piqued the investigators' curiosity, and they decided to apply for a search warrant for the Lignier home. Not long after, police arrived at the Lignier home in Vergeze commune with their search warrant. Immediately after entering the home, they found Richard's wife Francine and their daughter eating at the table. They did not acknowledge the officers, and as the raid went on, they continued eating as if everything going on around them was perfectly normal. Investigators were inclined to believe that the two were aware of what might have happened to Elodie Morel.

A thorough search of the home revealed that Elodie was no longer in the home, but there were signs that she had been there at some point. Police recovered a number of items belonging to Elodie, including a dressing gown, two pairs of shoes, a black top, and her phone. Investigators were now convinced that they had the right suspect in custody. Also recovered was a well-concealed revolver which had brownish stains on it, probably blood stains. When Mingaud was confronted by police about the gun, he did not react in any way, and offered no answers. He just stared at it like it had nothing to do with him. The evidence recovered led police to believe that something terrible had happened to Elodie. They arrested everyone in the home with the intention of sorting it all out at the police station.

Richard's Statement

At 8 p.m. on May 5, 2005, the defendants arrived at the police station, and were placed in separate interview rooms to prevent them from communicating. Investigators started with Mingaud's interview, but they soon realized that he was not interested in helping them. He maintained that he had met Elodie at the bar on May 2, and that he had picked up her bank card after she lost it. It soon became clear that Richard was the weakest link.

"I know you know. You know what happened. It wasn't you, but you know," one of the investigators told Richard. "Yes," he quickly replied, and began recounting the events following up to his arrest. He stated that Mingaud showed up at his home on May 1 at around breakfast time. He did this often, and he would lounge around the house like he owned it. He regaled the family with stories about his past as a notorious thug, and would take every opportunity to show off his knife and gun. That Sunday morning, Mingaud told Richard and Francine that he had been given a big contract by another prisoner, and that he would be paid €5,000 to kill someone. He then took out a pistol from his bag and showed it to the couple. He spent the day telling stories, and left the house at night. Richard stated: "After this conversation, he left my house at around 9 or 9:30 p.m. He got into his ZX car. I didn't see him again that night. He came back to my house on Tuesday, May 3."

Mingaud arrived at the house at around 6 a.m. on Tuesday morning, just as the Ligniers were having breakfast. He walked into the house with a gun in his hand, saying, "I've done something stupid." He then stated that his plan had gone wrong and that he needed a place to hide. "Look, I have a girl in the car, I need to use the garage." The Lignier's garage was about 500 meters from their home, and Richard agreed to Mingaud's request without asking any questions. Richard took Mingaud to the garage to open the door for him, and Mingaud drove his car inside. Richard told investigators, "I didn't see what was in the boot and I didn't hear anything." Mingaud then asked Richard for some plastic zip ties. Mingaud then stated that he would be sleeping in the garage to make sure the girl didn't shout. Richard left the garage and went back to his house and left for work. He came back later in the day and the family went about their routines like nothing had happened.

Francine's Statement

Francine was as forthcoming as her husband, and she told investigators, "At 6 p.m. Mingaud came back to the house. He asked for a bottle of water. The girl was thirsty. He told me that he had made her sniff the white powder. I understood that he had drugged her." After spending two hours in the garage, he had come back to the house for dinner. He had presents for the family – Elodie's belongings. He gave them a jumper, a dress, two pairs of shoes, and a mobile phone. He offered the items to their daughter, and neither Francine nor Richard asked any questions about it. He then told the family that he needed to get rid of the girl because she could incriminate him. "I asked him 'how can you kill her?' He made a strangling gesture and said 'like this,'" Francine told police.

Confession

When investigators confronted Mingaud with Richard and Francine's statements, he finally caved. He admitted to investigators that he had set up the casting call pretending to be a woman named Nicole Forestier. Part of the advert's description read, "The payment is €1,000 per day, with the hotel and restaurant paid by the production." He stated that when he received the email from Elodie, he was immediately struck by the thought, "Why not her?" He continued, "I called her, I gave her a meeting time for Monday, May 2 at the bar de l' escale in Aigues-Mortes." He told police that Elodie arrived at the bar at 6:30 p.m., and was surprised that she was meeting a man. Mingaud introduced himself as Forestier's assistant, and told her that they were going to visit the places where the shoot was going to take place.

Mingaud told investigators that his intention was only to steal Elodie's bank card and PIN. At 4:30 a.m., he had parked on a small road to carry out his plan, and that it was only then that he attacked her. He stated that Elodie had pushed him with her hand and he hadn't liked it, so he hit her. He then pushed her against the car on the passenger side, and she gave him her PIN. He told investigators that he let her go soon after. He maintained that he hadn't kidnapped her, and that he had no clue about her whereabouts. No one believed his story.

Additional Evidence

As investigators were interviewing Mingaud, officers were dispatched to search the Lignier's garage. Inside, they discovered even more evidence. There were footprints visible on the floor, cut cable ties, a bottle of water, more than 30 cigarette butts belonging to the same brand Mingaud was known to smoke, and traces of blood all over the floor. The grey ZX was in the garage, and inside they discovered a packet of white powder, and later analysis revealed that it was a mixture of crushed sedatives. The water bottle matched the one Francine Lignier had described to investigators, and the mouth of the bottle was swabbed. DNA analysis showed that it was a mixture of Mingaud's and Elodie's DNA, particularly Elodie's saliva and Mingaud's semen. 18 hours after Mingaud was taken into custody, investigators had finally finished collecting evidence.

Armed with the new evidence, investigators confronted Mingaud about his lies in the initial confession.

Second Confession

23 hours after he was taken into custody, Mingaud changed the details of his confession. He admitted to hiding his car in the Lignier's garage with Elodie in the trunk. He told investigators that his plan was to discuss keeping Elodie's bank card and then he would let her leave if she promised not to cause any trouble. He planned to tell her that he was just to kill time, and that he had let roam around the garage freely. They chatted and gossiped as she walked around. He maintained that he was not violent towards her, and that they finally came to an agreement – he would let her go free in return for her silence. As soon as dawn broke, he planned to drive her back to Aigues-Mortes to pick up her car and let her leave. However, this was when things took a turn for the worst.

He told investigators, "I said to her, 'you will take the steering wheel and drive me back to the parking lot. Then you can go home.' We got into the car at the same time and we bumped into each other. And then, I don't know what got into her but she tripped me." He then flew into a rage, grabbed a cord lying on the ground and strangled her. "I still don't understand why she tripped me," he added. Investigators saw no sign of remorse or regret as they watched Mingaud speak. They still had no idea where Elodie's body was, so they decided to flatter him to obtain more information. Finally, he told investigators that the body was in Elodie's BMW, which was in the parking lot at Aigues-Mortes cemetery.

Autopsy Results

The post-mortem examination results concluded that Elodie Morel's cause of death was strangulation. There were other visible bruised on her body – bruising on her head matched the butt of the handgun recovered in the Lignier home, there were cable tie marks on her wrists disproving Mingaud's claims that Elodie was roaming free in the garage, and her jumper and jeans had traces of blood and semen. The results also showed that Elodie had been drugged by the white powder recovered from Mingaud's car.

Despite the results pointing to sexual assault by Mingaud, he denied having any sexual contact with Elodie.

Sentencing

Richard and Francine Lignier were charged with complicity in the kidnapping and murder of Elodie Morel.

On January 28, 2008, the trial for the kidnapping and murder of Elodie began. Guillaume Mingaud was smiling in the court and maintaining eye contact with the jury as the trial progressed. He didn't try to defend himself, but told the court that Richard was the killer. Hearing this, Richard, who was also on trial for complicity, collapsed. The trial was suspended, to be resumed the next day. Richard showed up to court on a stretcher. Responding to Mingaud's accusation, the prosecution maintained that Mingaud was attempting to manipulate the jurors. The evidence was presented, with emphasis on Mingaud's DNA present on the bottle and Elodie's clothes. They specifically highlighted the mixture of Elodie's saliva and his semen on the bottle. Mingaud resorted to pushing outrageous claims, telling the court that he had fallen in love with Elodie and that he couldn't have hurt her. This claim sparked outrage from Elodie's family.

Richard and Francine Lignier were asked why they never intervened – a question that was on almost everyone's mind. Their response was that they didn't see anything, they didn't understand what was going on, so they didn't do anything.

After a five day trial, Richard and Francine Lignier were found guilty of complicity in kidnapping and ignoring the crime, and were sent to serve six years in prison. The prosecution appealed this sentence, and a year later, Richard and Francine's sentences were increased to eight years.

Guillaume Mingaud was sentenced to serve life in prison with a minimum of 20 years.

THE MURDER OF EMMA WALKER

BARBARA HUTTON

Most of us have seen a movie or some tv series on the trials and tribulations of college bullies and the popular football player and cute teenager cheerleader. Most of us have probably already formed some kind of perception on what type of people they are – rude; full of themselves; picking on others and generally a downright plague to those around them. But this was no movie or tv series and, Emma Walker was not any preconceived version of a typical college cheerleader – in fact she was the complete opposite.

Born on the 20th March, 2000 in the beautiful suburbs of Knoxville, Tennessee, Emma Jane Walker was a dedicated and fun-loving daughter to her parents, Jill and Mark Walker and supportive older sister to her younger brother, Evan. Emma had been popular in her community and not one to shy away from the limelight. But, at the same time and, through her solid loving upbringing, Emma was also a very well-grounded individual who went out of her way to help her community through volunteer work.

By the time Emma had started as a freshman at Central High School, she had already, at the young age of 14, fallen in love with a potential career in either caring for animals or, pursuing a pediatric nursing degree. With her beautiful long bouncy blonde hair and sparkling blue eyes, Emma Walker was the epitome of a striking young all-round American girl with a bright future ahead of her.

In her first year as a Freshman at Central High School, it wasn't long before she had made a number of friends and was picked as a Bobcats Cheerleader where she flourished with her own unique style and brand. Emma was a go-getter and full of high spirits with a wonderful sense of humor, so it wasn't long before she caught the eye of a good-looking quarter-back footballer, William Riley Gaul who immediately warmed to her witty outlook on life and stunning beauty. The two immediately hit it off and friends could see how it wasn't long before the two of them had become inseparable. Two years older than Emma, Riley Gaul presented a striking athletic pose at the young age of 16 and had his fair share of admirers and teenage ex-girlfriends in tow. But, for Riley, Emma quickly had become his first true love and within the first few months of their budding relationship, he had become potentially a little too obsessive for even Emma's parents own liking. In fact, within the first several months of the relationship, Emma's parents had noted a marked change in their daughter's well-being. From always being a bubbly outgoing and opinionated young girl, Emma had now seemed more distant and withdrawn, spending most of her spare time with her new boyfriend. What they were not aware of at the time, is that Riley had slowly and surely been eroding Emma's self- confidence over the months, drawing her closer to him for protection and, ultimately away from her family and friends.

There was nothing untoward about Riley Gaul, in fact, he was a well-adjusted student who was also popular and quite the jokester himself. Raised by his mother and grandparents, Riley excelled in school and enjoyed video games and had become an avid Star Wars fan – in other words, a typical teenage young man who also had a bright future ahead of him. Although Riley was quiet and kept mostly to himself, his football career had taken off and most of his coaches thought the young talented Gaul was destined to one day play for a team in the NFL.

By all appearances and photos, Riley and Emma seemed the perfect couple in love. But like all photos are a snapshot of just an orchestrated second, they were not in fact the happy couple they often portrayed. Emma and Riley's beaming smiles in pictures and on social media was, for most of the time, a far cry from reality. Even after the first year of their relationship, friends often had found them fighting with each other. Riley, although not physically abusive, did control Emma in all senses of the word. Friends of Emma recall how he was verbally cruel to her on more than just a few occasions and they too, had noted a change in their once lively and vivacious friend. But the relationship between the two struggled on and off for two years; Riley being somewhat of a player on and off the field, Emma would break off the relationship only to eventually get back together with Riley again in a matter of weeks. But Mark and Jill Walker were loving and concerned parents and so began to try limit the time their daughter was spending with Gaul. They went as far as to take her mobile phone away from her, but it wasn't long before Riley had purchased another in order for them to stay in contact. Over the two years, the relationship had developed into a type of toxicity that was unhealthy for both of them – Emma becoming more and more insecure and distant and, Riley becoming more possessive and aggressive.

Emma Walker, despite her troublesome bond with Riley, was powering full steam ahead with her career dreams and had settled on seeking a career as an NICU nurse, working and supporting young babies in a neo-natal ward. Emma still kept her passion for animals going though through her volunteer job at the local veterinarian clinic and animal welfare society. Emma headed off in the Fall of 2016 to her new college, keen to get her life back on track and having re-examined her difficult and toxic connection with Riley. Things came to a head quickly when Emma discovered photos on a social media website of Riley recently in the arms of his ex-girlfriend and called it quits on their relationship once and for all.

This was indeed a devastating blow to Gaul who, although happily playing the field with other young women, was still in a possessive and controlling frame of mind when it came to Emma. He was not about to lose her again and set out to win her back – any way he could.

In the week leading up to Emma Walker's fateful murder, Riley continued to text and harass her, calling her several times a day and leaving excessive amounts of text messages on her phone. But Emma was determined to carry on her life without Riley in it, ignoring the phone messages and telling him that it was over between the two of them when he called for what seemed, the hundredth time.

This of course fuelled Riley's obsessive nature to try even harder and, on the weekend of 18th November 2016, two days before Emma's death, he tried to lure her outside of her friend's house on the Friday evening, through faking his own kidnapping. Through using an unknown number, he sent Emma a series of texts stating that Riley had been kidnapped and that if she wanted to see him alive again, she was to come outside alone. After several of these creepy texts and staged phone calls, Emma eventually went outside with her friends, finding Riley lying outside on the ground dazed and acting confused. Everyone knew immediately that it was a hoax and Emma, emboldened by having her close friends around her, shouted at Riley to leave her alone for good and stormed back into the house.

The next day, Saturday, Emma drove home from her friend's house but, as she neared her driveway, she noticed a figure dressed all in black lurking on the pathway near her house. The man had his jacket hood up and she was unable to see his face. She quickly parked her car and went inside, locking the door behind her. Her fear was not abated when suddenly there was banging on the door and whoever it was, kept trying to forcefully open the door. Emma sent her friends a text telling them what was happening and how scared she was. Fearing for her safety, Emma picked up her phone again and sent the person who she had promised herself she would never speak to again a message. That message went to Riley and it said, "I still hate you, but I need you right now". Within minutes Riley called Emma back and immediately drove over to comfort his estranged girlfriend. Riley made a sweep of the property and checked the house to make sure there was no one around. But, if he thought he had won Emma over, he was about to come down hard. Jill Walker arrived home to find Emma and Riley on the front lawn. She got out the car and politely asked Gaul to leave. She did not want this young obsessive man in her daughter's life anymore. Emma agreed and rebuffed his advances and sent him on his way.

The rest of Saturday came and went and on the chilly Sunday, Emma finished her errands for the morning and went off to have some ice cream with her father. For the first time in a long time, Emma seemed her old cheerful self, laughing and joking around with her father that day. But that evening, Emma asked her parents to make sure the front door was locked securely that evening – the first time she ever asked them to. Emma totted off to her bedroom close to midnight that evening, crawled under the covers of her bed that was positioned against the wall and snuggled up for the night.

Around 2am on the morning of 21st November 2016, Emma's father was startled awake by a loud bang, followed quickly by the sound of another bang. It was the same noise as if someone had slammed a door shut. He scrambled out of bed and went to look around the house. Seeing nothing, he went first to his daughter's bedroom, opening the door to make sure she was okay. She was, he thought, fast asleep. He checked on his son and found the same. Puzzled, but thinking nothing more of it, Mark Walker climbed back into bed and fell sound asleep.

Jill Walker had set her alarm for an early rise that morning; she had errands to run and her daughter had a morning hair appointment that day. At 6.45am she went into Emma's room and touched her gently on the shoulder. "Time to wake up." But Emma didn't move. Jill tried again... and then again... and then more frantically. She felt for a pulse and couldn't find one. Hysterically calling 911, Jill and Mark couldn't comprehend how their daughter, who they had just said goodnight to a few hours ago, was no longer alive. Paramedics soon arrived at the pretty Knoxville suburb home and were unable to resuscitate Emma, initially thinking that it was a possible overdose. After all, there was a little blood on the pillow which may have been from vomiting, but otherwise no other signs or reasons evident for her death. It wasn't until Emma's lifeless body was taken to the hospital morgue that same morning, that a tiny head wound was discovered, the same size as a small bullet hole.

In the wall next to Emma's bed, a similar small hole was discovered – also the same size as a bullet entering from the outside. Investigators quickly scanned the garden and found two spent bullet casings in the grass. This was murder and they wanted their killer quickly. This was not a neighbourhood of drive-by shootings – this was quiet and peaceful Knoxville, no one gets shot and killed through their own bedroom wall.

That same morning, Riley Gaul woke from his slumber at his College some 20 miles away, to a barrage of text messages – condolences and heartfelt sympathies from friends all over. His heart breaking over the sudden agonizing news of Emma's passing, he posted on his Facebook page of his pain and grief – he had lost the love of his life and he would never get over it.

But as the hours of that first day wore on, Police heard from numerous community members and Emma's family of her estranged relationship with her ex, Riley Gaul. As they contacted friends of both Emma and Gaul, they began to formulate a picture of the toxic relationship that had endured over the past two years. Learning of the strange events over just this past weekend, detectives were keen to speak to Riley on his alleged kidnapping and on his whereabouts and movements over the past weekend.

Within minutes of police calling Riley in for questioning, it was clear to detectives that they were dealing with more than just a distraught ex-boyfriend. With Riley explaining the creepy and outlandish attempted – and unreported - kidnapping just a few days earlier, police became concerned on the language Gaul was using to describe someone he apparently loved. Consistently referring to Emma as 'the girl' instead of her name throughout his verbal statement, police pressed Riley on his whereabouts for the last 24 hours. He claimed that he had been by his dorm at college some 25 miles away and that he had spent most of the night sitting in his car in the parking lot crying over his break up with Emma. But police were not convinced. There was one thing that had come to light just minutes before their interview with Riley and that was a reported missing firearm by Riley's grandfather just a day before the killing. But with no weapon and no evidence – yet, they had to let Riley go.

With suspicion mounting, Riley became uneasy realizing that police were not on his side. He left the interview room and headed back to his dorm, contacting his two friends, Noah Walton and Alex McCarty for support. His friends had stuck with him and they knew him. They had shared the same interests and, despite his recent behavior, they had offered their concerns and condolences as he went through this difficult time in his life.

But if Noah and Alex thought Riley was a stand-up guy, they were about to find out that the person and friend they had known for many years, was in fact, a cold-blooded killer. Riley, in a phone call to his friends, confessed he had taken his grandfather's gun. But he intimated that his reasons were about his own safety after the kidnapping and that he had nothing to do with Emma's murder. In a separate phone call to another of his friends, Riley had separately asked if his friend knew how to remove fingerprints from a gun. On both of these occasions, all of Riley's friends had communicated with each other, growing more concerned at the behavior and actions Riley was exhibiting. But Riley's excuse for all his talk of the weapon was because he was now fearful that police would not believe him and that he needed to get rid of the weapon and needed their help.

Noah and Alex did not like this one bit, and bravely contacted the investigators on the team to tell them of what they had learned. It took more than just a little courage for the two of them to give evidence behind their long-standing friend's back. In fact, they would become more involved than ever and, pivotal to the arrest of Riley in the hours and days to come.

In a daring sting operation just 72 hours after Emma Jane Walker was murdered, Noah and Alex volunteered to be part of bringing Riley down and catching him red-handed in the disposal of the firearm used in the killing of Emma Walker. Police hatched a plan to rig Noah and Alex with undercover surveillance cameras and recording devices and set them up with a plan to get Riley to confess. Like a true Hollywood movie, Noah and Alex played their part masterfully, meeting up with Riley at their house and gently coaxing him to talk about Emma and the events of her death. Noah and Alex, using their hidden camera and recording device, managed to get Riley to talk openly about the gun and also captured his comments on him looking to dispose of the weapon. Riley, none the wiser, explained that he wanted to throw the gun in the Tennessee River where it was likely never to be found. His nonchalant attitude was glaringly obvious on the tape. Again, stating that he would never harm Emma, Riley's excuse for getting rid of the gun, was as implausible as his own alibi. Riley explained that, although he did not shoot and kill Emma, the fact that he had taken his grandfather's gun for his own protection, was the reason why police were after him. By getting rid of the gun, Riley believe the police would then have no reason to pursue him as a suspect. Organizing with his two friends, Riley made plans with Alex and Noah to dispose of the weapon the next evening when it was dark.

The following night, and as planned, the three of them took off for 'The Bluffs' near the Tennessee River; a gated complex that had a high access point to the river and where Riley could easily toss the weapon from the cliff, never to be seen again. This would have been the ideal spot to dispose of any evidence. Of course, Noah and Alex continued to play along as instructed, recording everything for the police. But before they made their way to The Bluff, Alex pulled the car into their favorite drive-thru restaurant, ordering him and his friends some take away meals and drinks before heading out to the location. For the Alex and Noah and, as they eventually testified in court, it was their way of saying 'goodbye' to the friend they once knew and, before the police would take Riley away for good.

As the three pulled their car up to The Bluffs and, before Riley was able to dispose of the weapon, police swooped in arresting Riley and taking the weapon away as evidence. Just 72 hours since Emma was cruelly and coldly murdered in her bed in the quiet pretty town of Knoxville, Riley was in custody and both the police and the community could breathe a sigh of relief.

It would take detectives and prosecutors just under two years to put their evidence and case together against William Riley Gaul and what had transpired in those dreadful cold early hours of 21st November 2016. For the prosecution, they had the evidence they needed for a full conviction and a charge of first-degree murder. The Cell phone towers near Emma Walker's home had placed Riley in the vicinity of the killing and not, at his university dorm many miles away as he had initially said in his interview. The police also now had the weapon which used the same caliber bullet as the one that was fired into Emma's bedroom wall and entered Emma's head with swift and deadly effect. And, above all, the police also had the testimony of his friends and the video footage of the undercover sting operation. This was a slam dunk according to prosecutors. But, on the first day of trial in May 2018, Riley's defense lawyer immediately put a grinding halt to their case.

Standing next to a changed Gaul, who sat rumpled, overweight and disheveled next to his Defense Attorney, Wesley Stone, the lawyer pleaded the jury to see the case as not murder in the first degree, but rather reckless homicide. For Stone, his client had not intended in any way to kill Emma Walker, but was rather, and feebly, attempting to win her back through a series of, albeit bizarre events. Admitting upfront, that Riley had fired the shots into the house, the defense attorney progressed with his argument stating how distraught Riley had been as a result of the break up and that he was trying to come up with a way where Emma would come running back to him. In his own warped mind, Riley had believed that if he scared Emma enough, she would turn to him for protection.

This was the reason for his inexplicable and peculiar actions that weekend, starting with his alleged kidnapping, followed by the attempted break in on the Saturday when Emma returned from her friend's house. So, on the Sunday night, Riley had waited outside her home and, when everyone had gone to sleep, he fired two shots into the wall, hoping that he would have the opportunity to come to her rescue.

But the truth is, no matter how you look at this case, the only logical conclusion is that the intention to control and, eventually kill Emma, is evident. And, this is what the prosecution argued. Emma and Riley had dated for a few years on and off. He had been around the home of Emma and her family so many times, it was without any doubt that he would have known exactly where Emma's bedroom was and, where her bed was in relation to the wall. His behavior and threatening texts were also brought into evidence. On many occasions, Riley had posted his hatred for Emma on social media and had sent her texts stating things like "I will look for you in the obituary". All of this pointed to a disturbed man who, on the surface had come across as a bright and caring young man, but underneath his violent verbal abuse had spun out of control.

When Emma had eventually found her feet and was now starting a new life without him, he had thought they would – as they had always done – get back together again. But this time it was final and despite his frantic attempts at attention, she had stood her ground. Enraged at his futile efforts to win her back, the prosecution determined that Riley had eventually given up and decided that, if he could not have her, then no one could. He took his grandfather's firearm; went to Emma's home; stood no more than a foot away from the wall of her bedroom and, fired a shot right where she lay. He knew he would have injured her at the very least – his actions were intentional – Emma's death, inevitable.

It took the jury no more than a few hours to come back with their verdict. Guilty. Not on reckless homicide, but murder in the first degree. Along with the sentence, William Riley Gaul was also found guilty on the counts of stalking, theft and possession of a firearm, tampering with evidence and reckless endangerment. Unemotional and unresponsive, Riley was taken away and eventually received the maximum sentence of 51 years in prison for his brutal crime. Riley will only be eligible for parole when he is the ripe old age of 71.

For Emma, her young potential life was stripped from her at the young age of 16. Beautiful and full of aspiring talent, Emma was to become a neo-natal nurse, saving lives and caring for new born infants. She was clever, pretty, goofy and full of energy as her friends described her. She met a young high school football player who was also young, talented and had a bright future ahead of him. But the warning signs as this poisonous relationship progressed, became more and more evident over the years to those closest to them. Watching the possessive nature and verbal abuse take place in front of them, it is hard to know why those around them did not step in sooner to help. Emma's parents had tried everything to wean their loving daughter from this terrible hold, yet Emma's own determination and addiction to Riley, placed her right in his firing line. Emma herself, kept returning back for more and brushed off the voiced concerns of her friends.

What transpired in this young couple's life is not a rare occurrence. It happens all too often.

THE VALENTINES DAY MURDER
ANA BENSON

Richard and Stacy Schoeck had a perfect marriage, or at least it looked ideal for their friends and family. Even though they have been together for a long time, they seemed to have eyes only for each other. Richard was Stacy's fifth husband and everyone was certain that he was indeed the love of her life. The couple still went on dates and celebrated their love in every way possible. So when Valentine's Day in 2010 came around, the Schoecks were setting up a romantic little getaway and a card exchange in a picturesque Belton Bridge Park which is located in Lula, Georgia.

Lula is a quiet little tourist town so when their Police Department received a frantic phone call with Stacy on the other end of the line, they knew something serious had happened. The town was shocked to discover that a murder occurred right there in their calm little oasis. But soon enough, the sinister plot started to unravel and the law enforcement realized that things were not as they seemed.

So what made Stacy Schoeck turn on her loving husband and who helped her with the murderous plan?

Early life

Stacy Morgan was born in 1971 in Florida. Her childhood wasn't perfect at all and her father died when she was really young. This left a permanent mark on Stacy even though her mother remarried soon and she did have a father figure in her life. She was also molested during this time frame by an individual who remained anonymous to everyone around her. Stacy grew up to be a lovely teenage girl who would fall in love easily. She met her first husband while she was still in high school and the couple got married shortly after. Unfortunately, he wasn't what Stacy was looking for and it took her two years to come to this conclusion. She filed for a divorce and the two separated.

When Stacy was twenty years old, she met her second husband. Soon after the wedding, Stacy found out that she was pregnant with her first child. The marriage lasted a little more than a year and she once again filed for a divorce when her son was just a toddler. Instead of being beaten down by two failed marriages, Stacy remained strong and made a decision to improve herself. After all, she was only twenty-two years old. She applied for college and got accepted. Stacy moved on to raise her son on her own and earn a degree in psychology and nursing at the same time.

She managed to find the employment as soon as she got out of college. Stacy was still very optimistic about her love life and wanted to find someone to spend the rest of her life with. She met her third husband in 1997 but unfortunately, the marriage was short-lived once again. It lasted for only six weeks. Stacy decided to date casually in the future and gave birth to her second son in 1998. She was still a single mother but this didn't seem to bother her at all.

Stacy did need to improve her financial status and she found a better job opportunity at a clinic which was located in Atlanta. The family moved over there and she was ready to start over. She got an excellent position at the hospital's administration with the possibility of even better promotion. She would assist the doctors on a daily basis with various tasks. Stacy was a successful and independent woman who was capable of taking care of her two small boys on her own.

But something was still missing and Stacy was longing for a partner who would be there for her. She was tired of casual encounters and needed some stability. So in 2001 she married for the fourth time and moved out to a small town near Atlanta. She got pregnant once again and gave birth to her third son. She lived in a large house with her fourth husband and it seemed that her life was absolutely perfect. Her boys were happy and they loved the suburban lifestyle. On the other hand, Stacy was still unhappy. Soon after the separation from her fourth husband in 2005, Stacy met Richard Schoeck, a graphic designer who was slightly older than her. He was a patient at the hospital where Stacy worked at the time. The two hit it off immediately.

Richard Schoeck was an adventurer who lived his life to the maximum. Stacy was immediately attracted to his positive attitude and passionate outlook. Richard accepted Stacy's sons like they were his own and would often organize family outings that included the entire family. She loved how different Richard was from all of her previous husbands and thought that she had finally found the one.

Unconcerned about Stacy's previous failed marriages, Richard still wanted to make their relationship permanent. The couple did get married in 2007 but the ceremony wasn't standard at all. Stacy and Richard eloped and told everyone about the wedding once they came back home. It was in Richard's nature to do something so spontaneous and Stacy adored him for that.

Richard became a stay at home dad after the wedding and he would form a close bond with Stacy's boys. He was very involved with their school and hobbies so he ended up adopting the youngest two. He really did accept this small family as his own and wanted the best for the boys. Everyone approved of Richard and Stacy's family hoped that she finally found the man of her life. Unfortunately, this marriage would end up tragically in just a couple of years.

The murder of Richard Schoeck

Prior to Valentine's Day in February of 2010, Stacy invited Richard on a small romantic getaway to the town of Lulu, Georgia. They were supposed to meet in Belton Bridge Park which is a secluded area near the town itself and exchange gifts there. This wasn't unusual for the Schoecks because they would often go on different adventures that were supposed to spice up their love life. The Police dispatchers received a frantic phone call sometime after the nightfall. Stacy was screaming that her husband was shot and robbed. He wasn't showing any signs of life.

The police arrived at the scene of the crime and sure enough, Richard's body was lying next to his pickup truck. The blood was both inside and outside of the vehicle which meant that several shots were fired. At least one bullet hit him while he was still in the driver's seat or getting out of the car. He crawled out, perhaps to run away or defend himself. The shooter continued firing the gun until they were certain that Richard was dead.

The investigators immediately closed off the area and examined the tire tracks which were visible in the surrounding mud. They noticed that the third vehicle was definitely there and that it left the scene of the crime prior to the arrival of Stacy. The law enforcement marked them as the evidence. However, there were some red flags that indicated that this wasn't a standard robbery. For instance, Richard's valet was still in the car and his jewelry was on him. Nothing was taken from the scene.

Stacy wasn't a suspect at the time but the police escorted her to the station in order to interview her and get as many details as possible. Lulu is a quiet town where crime rarely happens so the law enforcement couldn't zero in on any possible reason why Richard was shot. One theory suggested that he might have interrupted another couple at Belton Bridge Park because it was a common meeting ground for lovebirds who wanted to spend some time together outside of their homes.

The interviews and investigation

Once Stacy got to the station, she started talking. She was asked to explain what they were doing at the remote park and she admitted that they did have problems in their marriage. She thought this would be the perfect time to add some flare to their relationship. Since Richard was a stay at home dad and she had difficult work hours, the two simply couldn't get any alone time to spend with each other. She was becoming desperate and unhappy.

She quickly admitted to having an affair to the shock of everyone who was present in the interrogation room. Her lover was a fellow co-worker from the hospital who was significantly younger than Richard. His name was Juan and he was a complete opposite of Stacy's husband. She needed intimacy and she fell in love with someone else who could give her everything she craved for. Stacy even took her lover to Las Vegas just a couple of weeks prior to the murder of her husband.

The detectives were interested in the affair and started asking questions related to the possibility that Stacy wanted to get out of her marriage with Richard in order to be with her new man. Stacy told them that she did think about leaving Richard but that no particular plans were made. She knew how much her children loved him and getting a divorce would probably break their hearts. They focused on Stacy's lover but she quickly debunked their claims by saying that he is not violent at all and that she cannot imagine him being involved with anything involving guns or shooting.

But Stacy did say that Juan knew about the rendezvous in the park so the police decided to call him up for an interview the next morning. Juan seemed oblivious to the events that took place last night and he told the detectives that Stacy claimed her relationship with Richard was open. This meant that each of them had someone on the side. Juan didn't seem to be bothered by this arrangement at all so the investigators started doubting their possible theory. Plus, Juan had a solid alibi for the time of the murder because he was in another city.

They were left without any solid lead in this case so it was time to look a bit further and include as much aid as possible. The park is a fairly isolated place but there was a nearby cell phone tower that covered the entire area. The investigators knew that if a call was placed from that location on the night of the murder, they would have the number listed. And it turned out that this was a crucial move made by the investigators because it would lead them in the right direction.

The list of calls was short because that cell tower is not in an urban area. The detectives used the contact information which was stored in both Stacy's and Richard's phones and they tried to find the match. Stacy's phone had the number that was called sometime around the murder. The contact info itself stood out because it said Mr. Results. The investigators were slightly confused because they had no idea who this person was. But calling him up would probably shed some light on the events that occurred on Valentine's Day.

The police quickly identified the mystery man who was present at the scene of the crime that night. His name was Reginald Coleman and he worked as a private fitness instructor in Atlanta. Coleman was born in Philadelphia but his criminal past led him to move out from his hometown and try to start over in another state. He was incarcerated in the past but managed to clean up his act. Coleman was doing fine financially and owned a fairly popular gym. As far as the local police force knew, he was staying away from any type of crime.

Todd Woodten who would become Coleman's attorney during the trial said the following on his client: "Reginald was a true survivor. He was street-savvy and always had a hustle going on. He did a lot of things for youth, trying to keep them off the street and keep them safe."

Once the police managed to attain the call records from Reginald Coleman's cell phone, they found the number he had called from the Belton Bridge Park. The investigators thought they would see Stacy Schoeck's digits but they were surprised with their discovery. Coleman called another woman - Lynitra Ross. The detectives then realized that the whole plot was more complicated that they initially assumed and that there are more players involved with the murder of Richard Schoeck. So how did all of them fit together?

After speaking to Coleman's friends, the police found out that Lynitra Ross was his ex-girlfriend who would often resurface in his life. But there was another detail that connected Lynitra to the murder – she worked at the same hospital as Stacy Schoeck and two of them were really good friends. Stacy was Lynitra's boss and a landlord. Since there was a third set of tire marks on the scene of the murder, the detectives quickly determined that the model did not fit the tires on Reginald's car. This did sidetrack them a bit but they were still determined to find out what really happened.

The investigators were certain that they did, in fact, have their suspect and that was Stacy Schoeck. However, they still had to connect the dots so they dug even further into the phone records of those three. There was a message exchange on the night prior to the murder of Richard Schoeck between the three parties. However, the most interesting clue was Stacy's bank account which clearly stated that she sent a total of $10,000 to Lynitra's account which she passed along to Reginald.

The arrests

Since the topic of the third vehicle was still the big unknown, the police started going through all cars which were somehow related to Stacy, Lynitra, and Reginald. And soon enough they were onto something. Stacy did have one car which she sold soon after the murder. It wasn't registered to her but she did use it often in order to drive her relatives or get them groceries. They were surprised to find out that Stacy put their vehicle on the market but she told them that they will get a newer model as a gift from her.

The police became very suspicious of this story so they tracked down the new owner and took a look at the tires as well as the insides of the car. And yes, the tire marks matched perfectly. Stacy Schoeck borrowed that car to Reginald Coleman on that fatal Valentine's Day. The evidence against Coleman was piling up and he was arrested on May 25th, 2010. But as soon as the interrogation started, he denied any involvement with Stacy Schoeck or the murder of her husband.

Lynitra Ross was arrested a couple of hours after Reginald but she also refused to provide the investigators with any useful information. It was time to pick up Stacy as well so the police arrived at the medical center she worked at and led her straight to the station. The investigators had plenty of circumstantial evidence to accuse her of the murder and they didn't have to wait for her accomplices to start talking about the crime. All three of them were in custody and it was time to face the justice for their actions.

Psychological assessment

Stacy Schoeck was put through a psychological assessment prior to the trial itself in order to determine if she had any underlying problems which were unknown to her or her family. The murder was well planned so she clearly wasn't distraught at the time which meant that Stacy knew exactly what she was doing when she asked her friend Lynitra to help her get rid of her husband.

The psychologists took a closer look at her prior relationships and marriages which ended in divorce. The reason for her unhappiness might lay in the fact that she lost her biological father when she was young and she was unable to connect to anyone. Not to forget that Stacy was also molested when she was just a child.

It was obvious that Stacy Schoeck was manipulative and knew how to get exactly what she wanted in every situation. Her intelligence was obviously high because she did put herself through school and successfully earned her degrees. However, her actions towards Richard Schoeck show that Stacy was also a sociopath because she hired a man to murder her husband and continued to live her life as nothing happened.

She mourned her husband publicly and got very emotional in front of her friends and family every time they saw her. The fact that she selected Valentine's Day as the date of the execution speaks volumes about her cold-heartedness towards Richard Schoeck.

The trials of Ross and Coleman

The first of three to stand a trial was Lynitra Ross. She entered the courtroom in May 2012 and was facing charges for a murder. After all, she was a co-conspirator who helped Stacy Schoeck find the hitman who would eventually pull the trigger and take Richard's life. Stacy was also present in the courtroom but she wasn't the accused in this situation. As a matter of fact, she testified on the side of the prosecution.

Stacy Schoeck was cooperating with the law enforcement and made a deal regarding her sentencing. She did everything to avoid the death penalty and was ready to talk about the murder of her husband. It was clear that her deeds were out in the open and she said the following as she took the stand: "I'm going to testify truthfully for Richard. It's all I can give his mom and his family and the children — all I can give them is the truth."

The jury then heard the story about the murder plot. Stacy Schoeck had the idea to take her husband's life in December 2009 after she noticed that her boys were acting strangely. They were getting into troubles and she started to suspect that they might be victims of molestation. She remembered how she behaved during the time she was assaulted as a child and found the connection. Of course, her first suspect was Richard because he was always with the boys.

Stacy also said: "I was just so fixated in my mind that Richard was doing something wrong that I said, 'I don't want the cops, I don't want a divorce, I want him dead.'" She then admitted to asking an unnamed man to help her kill her husband but he stopped returning her calls. Then she talked to her friend and co-worker Lynitra Ross and told her about her suspicions. Lynitra responded with the suggestion that they talk to her ex-boyfriend who would know what to do because he was "an experienced hitman".

After Lynitra Ross contacted Coleman, the two woman drove to his house and sat down with him in order to agree on some finer details regarding the hit. They talked and ate food from Zaxby's. Stacy suggested the park as the perfect place for executing her husband because he wouldn't suspect a thing. Reginald and Stacy agreed on the amount of money she would pay him for the murder, as well as on the vehicle he would take to the park. All three of them went to Belton Bridge Park so that Stacy could show him the exact place where her husband will be waiting.

Stacy noted in her testimony the following: "The only times I ever saw or spoke to Reginald Coleman was the day we had Zaxby's that afternoon and the following Saturday when we went up to Belton

Bridge. Everything else was done through Lynitra." She also added that she had given Lynitra the property she was renting to her as the payment for the help.

Lynitra's defense lawyers took the stand and told the jury that Stacy's testimony which involved the molestation claims was slightly off due to the fact that she admitted to having an affair in the first interview she gave after the murder. She didn't mention anything related to the possible sexual abuse of her children.

In August of 2012, Lynitra Ross was sentenced to life in prison. There would be no possibility of a parole either. Even though she didn't pull the trigger, she was the person who set up Stacy and Reginald to meet. Therefore, she was directly involved in the murder plot.

It was later determined that Richard Schoeck didn't have anything to do with child molestation but Stacy's plan was already completed and her husband was dead. The investigators took her claims seriously and talked to the middle boy who immediately said that he never accused Richard of anything. As a matter of fact, he never even talked to his mother about the alleged abuse. However, this didn't stop Stacy's attorneys from building their case around this.

Reginald Coleman's trial didn't last long because as soon as he appeared in front of the judge in November of 2012, he pleaded guilty to the murder of Richard Schoeck. He also faced charges for owning the firearm as a convicted felon. Stacy Schoeck was set to testify against him as well, which meant providing the courtroom with the full account of Reginald's actions.

Reginald Coleman agreed to kill Richard Schoeck after he heard the story of the alleged molestation directly from Stacy and Lynitra. Since he grew up in foster care, he often listened to the stories from his friends about their own abuse. Coleman thought that he could help the boys have a normal childhood by eliminating the threat from their life. He pleaded guilty in order to avoid the death penalty which was already on the table if he went on a trial. Coleman received the punishment of life in prison without the possibility of a parole and some additional years for the possession of the firearm.

Stacy Schoeck's trial

Once Ross and Coleman received their sentences, it was time for Stacy to appear in court for her own trial. The proceedings began in December of 2012 at Hall County Courtroom. Since Stacy cooperated with the prosecution in the trials of Coleman and Ross, the death penalty was off the table. Judge Jason Deal listened to the witnesses who described Richard Schoeck as a loving father and an exceptional friend who would never harm anyone. Stacy's defense attorneys once again repeated the story of the alleged abuse and claimed that her actions were severe because she wanted to protect her children from the aggressor.

When Stacy took the stand, she admitted to the crime and asked the judge to give her mercy. The defense told the courtroom about Stacy's own abuse and that she was acting erratically. However, the fact that the murder was planned months before it happened painted a picture of someone who wanted to eliminate her husband. Stacy had plenty of time to make sure that Richard was really the abuser and contact the law enforcement but she failed to do so.

Stacy's lawyers asked Judge Deal to consider giving Stacy a possibility of a parole and to keep in mind her troubled past. They also pointed out that Stacy was behaving well in prison and that she deserves a second chance. However, she received the punishment of life in prison without a chance to get out after serving thirty years which was the primary goal of her defense team.

Attorney Lee Darragh who led the prosecution said: "Judge Jason Deal appropriately recognized that Stacey Schoeck was the engine that put this train in motion, until the death of her husband. Without her involvement, this would not have occurred." The courtroom was filled with emotions because a large number of Richard's friends showed up for the hearing. One of the saddest moments was when Stacy's mother read a note which was written by her youngest boy which said: "I miss her every hour of every day, just like Daddy Richard."

Initially, Stacy Schoeck and Lynitra Ross were placed in two separate prisons in order to avoid any possible conflicts between the two but they were soon moved to the same facility – Pulaski State Prison. Stacy's family was left to wonder what was really the reason for this heinous crime because the exact motive was never uncovered. They got the custody of Stacy's three sons.

THE MURDER OF ASHLEY FALLIS

SARAH THOMPSON-CARLOS

What reason would a perfectly happy and healthy 28-year-old mother of two have for taking her own life? That is the question that seems to perpetually surround the case of Ashley Fallis, who was found dead of a bullet wound in the early morning hours of New Year's day in 2012. A beautiful young woman, Ashley was small and slight, with a bright smile and an attractive face. A photo of herself on her wedding days shows her kneeling it the grass with her children: her two daughters, Madelynn and Jolie, and her son, Blake. Her blond hair is elegantly pinned back off her face, and there's such joy on her face. It's hard to imagine that this young woman, so vibrantly fully of life, would take her own life and leave behind her three children, all under the age of 10 at the time of her death.

According to statistics gathered by the CDC, over half of American women who are killed have relations to intimate partner violence. After analyzing the murders of women in 18 different states, spanning across the years of 2003 to 2014, the CDC focused on exactly 10,018 different female deaths. Of all of those deaths, 55% of of them were related to intimate partner violence. Intimate partner violence can be described as family members, lovers, boyfriends, partners and spouses. That that definition in mind, even more chilling was the finding that in 93% of those cases, the perpetrator was a romantic partner, either current or former. It becomes even more unnerving to find out that 54% of those deaths were gun deaths.

It draws the question, with a statistical trend like this, is it possible that an otherwise happy woman, with her husband and children, would take her own life? Despite what her friends and family knew about her, was it possible that Ashley Fallis was hiding a secret depression so deep that she took a gun to herself to end it all?

Most people can't say that they married their high school sweetheart, but Ashley was one of the lucky few who could. Unfortunately, that relationship didn't last. They married soon after their high school graduation, and had two daughters: Madelynn and

Jolie. Despite the children, the marriage crumbled and fell apart, and the two divorced. It was in 2007 that Ashley met Tom Fallis, who would surely change her life. Tom Fallis was a responsible man, and he seemed to have his life together.

It was only one month into their new, budding relationship that Ashley fell pregnant once again. That was how Blake was brought into the family. Their son was what brought Ashley and Tom together, despite the shortness of their new relationship. It was only two weeks after Blake was born that Ashley and Tom decided to make their family official. Tom adopted Madelynn and Jolie, and they couple married.

As beautiful a story as it seems, Ashley's family felt as if the whole thing was moving quite quickly. After all, Ashley and Tom had only known one another for a month before she fell pregnant. Perhaps their relationship had grown closer throughout her pregnancy, and then after the birth of their son. Still, it was mostly unknown to Jenna Fox, Ashley's mother, and Joel Raguindin, Ashley's adoptive father. Ashley and her mother were extremely close, much more like friends than mother and daughter. Raguindin explained how they had tried to talk Ashley out of it before the wedding.

Tom Fallis seemed like an alright guy, at first. After all, he was ready to start a family. He seemed to have his life together. But, slowly, Ashley's family began to notice that there was something wrong with him. Tom Fallis had a problem with needing to be right all the time. He was aggressive, and seemed to always be ready to argue. Jenna Fox noticed it, and she didn't like it. Ashley's family was worried by the way Tom was acting, but there seemed to be nothing to draw the couple away from one another.

After the wedding, Ashley and Tom decided to settle down together with their three children in the small town of Evans, Colorado, just an hour outside of Denver. Tom took a jobs as a corrections officers at the Weld County Sheriff's Office, stationed at a local prison. Meanwhile, Ashley began working as a respiratory therapist. Those who knew Tom Fallis thought that he took the job as a corrections officer to feed his ego. After all, he was an aggressive person, according to Jenna Fox. He was also insecure. "He wanted total control of her," Jenna Fox told 48 Hours.

Jenna Fox also felt that she was a threat to Tom. After all, she was one of the only people that he could not isolate Ashley away from. The bond before mother and daughter was, seemingly, stronger than the bond between new husband and wife. The pressure to keep a balance between her new family with Tom and her relationship with her parents was put on Ashley. That pressure only increased when Blake, only just a toddler, was diagnosed with a brain condition. The condition was chronic, and would start to require almost all of Ashley's attention. Ashley was a doting mother, and did all that she could to give her son the attention and help that he required.

The constant attention that her son required, paired with the stress of Tom's increasingly controlling behavior was starting to take it's toll. Ashley was quite anxious, and overwhelmed with the situation as a whole. Still, Fox and Raguindin had never once suspected that Ashley was particularly depressed, nor did they suspect that she was suicidal. It just didn't seem like their daughter.

Still, Ashley and Tom's marriage was starting to feel the weight of that pressure. The two were considering a divorce, but apparently their relationship was slowly getting better as the holidays approached. The couple were planning a New Year's Eve party. And beyond that, they had received happy news. As the holidays closed in, Ashley had thought that she'd become pregnant again. They suspected that their family was about to grow even more.

That happiness only lasted so long. After she had gotten that positive pregnancy test, Ashley had stopped taking any medication just in case. After all, false positives happened all the time, and she wanted to make sure that whether the pregnancy was legitimate before she continued on. However, the day of their New Year's Eve party came and

Ashley began to bleed. Perhaps she had simply not been pregnant at all, or perhaps she was miscarrying. Whatever the cause of her bleeding, Ashley had been excited for the new baby. Learning that she was no longer pregnant caused her some significant sadness.

Despite learning that she wouldn't be a new mother once more, Ashley and Tom went forward with their New Year's Eve party all the same. After all, the invitations had been made, and the guests were on their way.

The part was a disaster. Jenna Fox describes the way that the tension between herself and her daughter's husband was becoming almost unbearable. Fox told 48 Hours that she "knew that Tom hated me". Despite the friction between mother-in-law and husband, the party was beginning to wind down without major incident - that is, until Tom Fallis went into a blinding rage because he had overheard Ashley's uncle offering her some marijuana. He began to swear, furious and loud. He told her that she didn't need to get high, even if she was still upset about the miscarriage. He told her, "It happened," and then told her that they were leaving, and to "Fuck everybody," and just let it go.

As Ashley's parents were leaving the party, they observed as Tom went into the bedroom, slamming the door behind him. Ashley walked them out, and they said their goodbyes at 12:04 am, after the New Year's ball had already dropped. Fox didn't observe anything out of the ordinary about her daughter. She didn't seem upset by Tom's behavior, after all. It wasn't out of place for Tom to act like this, and become enraged and swear. As Fox and Raguindin hugged their daughter and said their goodbyes on the front porch, they had no idea that this would be the last time that they saw their daughter alive.

Ashley isn't here any longer to tell us the rest of her story. What we know of that night is what Tom Fallis claims happened, and the autopsy reports, and the police records. As they guests filtered out of the house, they were among the last to see Ashley Fallis alive. When the last guest left and the door closed, no one but Ashley and Tom Fallis really know what happened that night that lead to the death of Ashley early in the hours of New Year's Day.

According to Tom Fallis, Ashley came into the bedroom in a defiant mood, and he said that she told him that if she wanted to get high, then she would get high. Tom told police that he told her to do whatever she wanted. Tom told the police that he had been in their closet, getting changed, when he heard the sound of her loading a gun across the room. Supposedly, it was the .9mm Taurus that Ashley kept under her mattress. As Tom walked out of the closet, he asked her what she was doing - and then, he heard the sound of a gunshot. Tom claims that he ran across the room to where Ashley was and held her head where the gunshot wound was, then grabbed the phone and dialed 911.

A recording of Tom Fallis' panicked 911 call plays Tom's voice, panicked and screaming: "My wife just shot herself in the head! Please help me! Please help me!" While the 911 operator tries to get his exact location and calm him down, Tom's voice comes through the call, tinny and screaming: "Ashley, no! Ashley, no!"

Finally, as the 911 operator tries to get more information, Tom can be heard shouting at his dying wife: "You are not leaving me! You are not leaving me! Stay right here!"

All in all, Ashley's family had only been gone for ten minutes. Ten minutes previous, Ashley had been on the porch, saying goodbye to all of her loved ones after celebrating the incoming of the new year. Her parents weren't even home, yet. They were still on the road when they saw the squad cars that were dispatched due to the call made by Tom.

At the hospital, Jenna Fox told 48 Hours that she knew, from the moment that she had seen her daughter lying in the hospital bed, that Tom Fallis had been involved. Perhaps it was a mother's intuition. Whatever the reason, Fox had no doubt that her daughter wouldn't have committed suicide. Even with the grief of her miscarriage hanging heavy over her that New Year's Eve, she was surrounded by her family and loved ones. Fox didn't believe for one second that suicide was an option for her daughter.

Ashley Fallis hadn't died immediately from that gunshot wound. She arrived at the hospital with severe trauma to the brain. But she wouldn't recover. The last time that her parents saw her alive and sentient was on the porch, ten minutes before she took a gunshot wound to the head.

But what happened? Tom's versions of events are clear. Ashley came into the bedroom, angry, and took a gun to her own head. Despite the fact that statistics put female suicides by firearm at only 31.2% (compared to male suicide by firearm at 56.4%), is it possible that Ashley had chosen such method? Women who commit suicide are often going to chose a less painful method, and one that would not leave behind such a mess. Pills and cutting of the wrists are much more popular methods when it comes to women who take their own life. But perhaps it was Ashley's grief that had driven her to take her own life with the gun she kept under her mattress.

Was it?

Despite the fact that Tom Fallis called in a suicide to 911, the police thought that it was important to question him about what happened. The police brought Tom Fallis into the station early on the morning of New Year's day, leaving his parents to watch his and Ashley's three small children. While Tom's frantic 911 call had seemed genuine, the police weren't all too sure. Neighbors had reported that they could hearing yelling and arguing coming from the couples house. Being questioned by Detective Rita Wolf, Tom was immediately put under scrutiny. The wound on Ashley's head was near the back. When told that her wound wasn't consistent with a suicide shot, Tom simply replied, "Bullshit! I didn't shoot my wife."

When investigators searched Tom's body, they found scratches on his chest, which he had said were from himself itching at his newly shaved chest. But that's not all investigators found. When they went into the Fallis' residence to take stock of the scene of the suicide, they discovered something strange. Tom's version of events had Ashley coming into the bedroom in an agitated state, then simply going across the room to retrieve her gun from under her mattress and shoot herself in the head. The state of the house, however, was inconsistent with that story.

Investigators found that pictures had been strewn from their place on the wall. It looked as if there had been a struggle. Not only that, but divorce papers had been found placed in a drawer. Tom Fallis had insisted that things had been going alright with him and Ashley, and that while they had been struggling before, things were moving in the right direction. The mere presence of divorce papers seemed to speak volumes, going against what Tom Fallis claimed was going on in his supposedly happy family.

At the hospital, Ashley Fallis had bruises on her legs. All of the evidence that investigators were digging up seemed to show that something else had gone down after all the guests had left the party - and that it wasn't suicide. Still, even after Tom Fallis was questioned for hours, he was released later that morning without charges being pressed against him.

Raguindin told 48 Hours that he and Fox were "shocked that they let him go." Even more shocking was what happened after that. Detective Wolf had told Tom Fallis that she didn't believe that Ashley could have inflicted that gunshot wound on herself. The position of the wound at the back of her head wasn't consistent with a suicide. Still, on January 5th, the coroner made an official ruling, and Ashley's death was listed as a suicide. Officially, the case was closed.

That seemed to be that. Ashley Fallis, wife, mother of three and devoted caretaker of her special needs son, was said to have taken her own life in the early morning hours of January 1st, ten minutes after waving goodbye to her family on the front porch after their New Year's Eve party.

The story for Tom Fallis, however, would go on. He packed up his children and moved them to Indiana, where he would attend graduate school. Despite the stress and strain of the relationship between Tom and Ashley's parents, they were determined to keep in contact with him for the sake of continuing a relationship with their grandchildren. After all, they were the only pieces of their daughter that they had left.

Life went on. For two years, Ashley's parents mourned their daughter's untimely death, and maintained a relationship with a man that they hated for the sake of their grandchildren. It seemed like no one else believed that Ashley wouldn't have taken her own life, and no one else believed that Tom Fallis was at fault. Until, one day, two years after Ashley's death, a man named Justin Joseph caught wind of the case. Joseph was a television news reporter with a source in law enforcement. Turns out, Ashley's parents weren't the only ones who were perturbed by the case.

Two years had passed, but Joseph took on investigating Ashley's story, anyway. Nothing seemed to sit right, and it was finally time to bring Ashley the justice that she deserved. Months were put into interviewing neighbors and friends who had already been cleared by the police, all of their statements taken and their concerns brushed off. In April of 2014, Joseph interviewed one of the Fallis' next door neighbors, Nick Glover, and found just what he needed to bust the case of Ashley's death wide open again.

Glover's versions of events differed from Tom Fallis'. According to Glover, he had heard Tom come out of the house, so he knelt down beneath the window sill to stay out of sight while he listened. Tom's parents were outside, and Glover could hear Tom saying, "Oh my god, I can't believe I did it." When his parents pressed him for more information, Glover heard Tom say: "I shot her." Of course, this wasn't the first time that Glover had told someone what had happened. In fact, the day that he was questioned by Evans Police, Glover told exactly the same thing to a Detective Michael Yates.

Glover's mother, Kathy Glover, had gotten a phone call that night from another neighbor by the name of Chelsey Arrigo. She told them to call the police, because she was sure that Tom Fallis had just shot his wife. Arrigo had heard Ashley yelling for Tom to get off of her, and the pop of the gun.

Everyone seemed to know what happened that night, and nothing was done. In fact, Detective Yates hadn't even written the report correctly. In his report of the incident that night, he quoted Arrigo as saying Ashley shot herself, not that Tom Fallis had shot her. Yates had also claimed that Glover had never told him about overhearing Tom admit to the murder of his wife. With contradicting statements, no one knew why a follow-up hadn't been given. Arrigo hadn't even been interviewed, despite knowing that Kathy had been in contact with her the night of Ashley's death. The case had been handled poorly from open to close, and no one seemed to know why.

Joseph found another person who had heard Tom Fallis admit the the murder of his wife: a sheriff's deputy who happened to be at the scene. It wasn't until two years later that he came forward to tell the investigators what he head heard. It's unclear as to why the case of Ashley Fallis wasn't treated as a homicide, or why no one seemed to take Glover seriously when he had told them what he heard, or why the sheriff's deputy said nothing to anyone until two years after the fact.

Was it a cover-up by the police? Or was it simply serious human error that caused the police not to go back and re-interview the people who had said they heard Tom Fallis admitting to murder? It seems hard to believe that the police would simply brush away Detective Wolf pointing out the position of the gunshot wound on Ashley's head, and two witnesses who had heard Tom Fallis saying clearly, "I shot her." One would want to hope that it was a serious error, and not the police deliberately looking the other way. There's no explanation for why Ashley Fallis' death was ruled a suicide, despite the evidence of a struggle in their house, and the witnesses that described Tom Fallis has raging and angry that night.

Whatever the reason that Ashley's case was closed, it was Justin Joseph that got it re-opened. His investigating opened up some serious questions about that night, and why the police had moved forward to rule her death a suicide. The case was reopened by a Evans, Colorado neighbor, Fort Collins, along with their much larger police force.

Tom Fallis had more information for the police, too. Two years after Ashley's death, Tom Fallis came forward during the new investigation with a suicide note that Ashley had supposedly written. There were several notes, one which read: "Dear Tom [...] I'm sorry for your pain. [...] I am a failure at everything." Of course, the timing of the suicide notes were suspicious. If Ashley had committed suicide, wouldn't the notes have shown up that first night?

Finally, it seemed like justice for Ashley Fallis was going to happen. In November of 2014, a grand jury made the decision to indict Tom Fallis for the murder of his wife. He was arrested in Indiana, and his children were put under the care of his parents. Tom Fallis had gotten away with putting his wife's supposed suicide in the past for almost three years. It wasn't until March of 2016 that Tom was finally put on trial.

The defense used Ashley's history of mental illness, anxiety, and the pain of her miscarriage to build a case against a dead woman. They claimed that it was Ashley who had shot herself in the middle of a crisis that early morning on New Year's Day. They pointed out that Ashley had been drinking at the party, and that there was even a history of suicide in her family: her uncle's mother and brother both died from suicide by gunshot. Was this just another suicide in a long line of tragedies? The defense seemed to think so.

Still, when Ashley's therapist took the stand, he made it clear that he did not consider Ashley a danger to herself or others. Still, Ashley was on medications from other doctors that she didn't tell her therapist. Defense used that against her, and in favor of Tom - saying it was entirely possible that Ashley Fallis could have written those suicide notes without telling her therapist.

When Ashley's parents were finally able to take the stand, they insisted that Ashley was fine throughout the night. Despite her miscarriage earlier in the day, Ashley was among family and friends. Her demeanor only changed when Tom became volatile. Jenna Fox described, once more, how Tom Fallis swore at them all and wished for them all to die before going into the bedroom and slamming the door.

Nick Glover also took the stand, repeating what he heard outside of his window that night. Tom Fallis' parents, however, denied that Tom had told them that he shot his wife. Kathy Glover also reiterated the phone call she got at one in the morning from Chelsey Arrigo. Unfortunately, when Arrigo took the stand, she couldn't remember making such a statement to Kathy Glover. All she remembered was hearing some arguing. Apparently, Arrigo was intoxicated because of her own New Year's celebration. Weld County Sheriff's Deputy, Chris Graves, was able to testify that he also heard with Nick Glover had heard that night, which was Tom Fallis admitting to shooting his wife. Still, he was questioned pretty hard after admitting that he should have come forward about it sooner than two years after the fact.

Forensic evidence didn't fair well in Ashley's favor, either. It was determined that the gunshot would very well could have been self inflicted. And yet, the prosecution called forward a forensic expert of their own, Jon Priest, who explained the exact opposite: no, Ashley's gunshot wound could not have been self inflicted.

There was so much testimony and evidence that the jury had to go through. The conflicting theories from the defense and the prosecution told two entirely different stories about what happened that night to Ashley Fallis. When the Jury retreated to deliberate the case and make their verdict, it didn't take them very long. In fact, the jury was only out for about three and a half hours. When they finally came back, Ashley's family could only wait with baited breath as the jury read out their decision.

Not guilty.

Tom Fallis was acquitted on the murder of his beloved wife, mother of his children. Ashley's family still holds their opinion that their daughter would never take her own life, and Justin Joseph maintains that the entire case of Ashley's death was handled poorly from start to finish. There was reasonable doubt that Ashley had killed herself that night, and there was no follow up done. Still, even after all the evidence was presented, the jury could not find Tom Fallis guilty. Whatever happened to Ashley Fallis that night will only ever be known by two people: Ashley and Tom.

THE MURDER OF BROOKE WILBERGER

OLIVIA WATSON

Chapter 1

May 24, 2004 is a day many people in Corvallis, Oregon will never forget. It was the day a drunk man who was also high on crack set forth to destroy a life. Joel Courtney set out that morning in his 1997 green Dodge Caravan in search of a young, pretty co-ed to fulfill his dark fantasies. He cruised through the Oregon State University campus, searching, failing. But Courtney was persistent, and his wishes were soon fulfilled after he came across the Oak Park apartment complex a block down the road.

On the same morning, Brooke Wilberger woke up without any inclination that this might be her final day on Earth. She was newly home after finishing her first year of University, and was enjoying how sunny the spring had turned out to be. She headed over to the Oak Park apartment complex, which her sister managed, to help do some cleaning and basic repairs. Her sister needed help washing the lightposts out in the parking lot, so Wilberger grabbed some rags and a bucket of soapy water and got to work.

A few minutes into her work, Wilberger noticed a green van pull up. Inside, a man was waving an envelope at her, trying to get her attention. He looked like he needed help, so Wilberger approached. When the van pulled away seconds later, all that was left of Brooke was the soapy water and her now-broken flip flops.

It would be more than five years before Brooke Wilberger came home, but she would never come home alive. The story of her disappearance was a twisted tale full of hope, but it would only ever have a bittersweet ending.

Chapter 2

Brooke Wilberger was born in Fresno, California on February 20, 1985. She was the youngest of six. With three older sisters and two older brothers, she lived in a busy household, but it was a pleasant place to live. Her parents, Greg and Cammy Wilberger, were devout

Mormons, and raised their children to be the same. The family was incredibly close-knit.

Brooke Wilberger grew to be quite a beautiful, accomplished young woman. Besides boasting a strong set of mormon morals, she also excelled in school and had a lot of friends. The tall, thin blonde also received a lot of attention from the guys in her school, but she seldom dated.

The summer before Brooke began high school, the Wilberger family left California behind and moved North to Eugene, Oregon. Here, Brooke attended Elmira High School, and met her first serious boyfriend, Justin Blake. Blake also came from a mormon family, and was devoted to his religion, so the couple got along famously. They respected each other's minds, bodies, and faith.

The young couple graduated together in 2003, and while they were both dedicated to each other, they were on different paths towards the future. Wilberger wanted to go right to college so she could better equip herself with the knowledge she would need to turn around and better those in need around her. Blake was ready to jump into missionary work.

Wilberger was accepted into the Brigham Young University in Provo, Utah, and when she set off for her freshman year there, Blake set off for Venezuela to participate in a Mormon missionary campaign.

Although she was separated from her first love, Wilberger could not deny how happy she was at Brigham Young. The University was owned and operated by the Church of Jesus Christ of Latter Day Saints, and was the largest religious university in the country. She was immersed in her faith in new experiences and knowledge. She was actively participating in something much larger than herself, and she loved it.

Wilberger kept in constant contact with her family while away at University. She would often call and tell them about what she was learning, who she was meeting, and what she was doing. Her favorite topic of conversation, though, was always the inspiration her surroundings gave her to do better for the world. Although she was excited to see her family after the end of the year, she was in no rush to leave the busy, bustling campus for small-town Oregon.

After finishing her classes for the year, Brooke returned home to her family in late April of 2004. Her parents still lived in Eugene, but she wanted to maintain some of her freedom, so Brooke often stayed with her sister, Stephanie, who lived an hour outside of Eugene in an apartment complex she managed in Corvallis.

Her family were ecstatic to have her back home, close by, where they believed she would be safe.

Chapter 3

On May 24, 2004, Brooke had been home for about a month. She was staying with her sister in the Oak Park apartments, which were just down the road from Oregon State University, where summer classes were already in full swing.

That morning, a female student of Oregon State named Randy was walking through the Reser Stadium parking lot when she noticed a green van driving around her. When it pulled up next to her, the driver of the van got out and asked Randy for directions. The student had a bad feeling about the man, and when she looked in the back seat of the van she noticed a bunch of empty boxes and blankets. Before the man could get too close, Randy excused herself and hurried off to class.

Several minutes later, another student, Crystal, was approached by the same van in the same parking lot. Crystal did speak to the man, who again asked for directions, but the conversation was interrupted by an athletic's coach, who Randy had reported the earlier incident to. When confronted by the coach, the van's driver quickly jumped back into his vehicle and sped off of the campus.

While this was all happening, Brooke Wilberger was a block down the road from Reser Stadium at the Oak Park apartment complex. That morning she was planning on helping her sister Stephanie do some routine maintenance work on the complex. She decided to start with washing the lamp posts in the parking lot, so she grabbed a bucket, filled it with soapy water, and headed outside. Stephanie saw Brooke hard at work scrubbing the lamp posts at 10:00 a.m. It was the last time she ever saw her sister alive.

Shortly after 10:00 a.m., the same green van that had been causing havoc on the Oregon State campus pulled into the Oak Park apartment complex. The van pulled up to Brooke, blocking her view of the apartments. He began asking for directions, but when Brooke drew near, he pulled out a knife and forced the 19-year-old into the back seat of his van and sped away.

Five minutes down the road, the van pulled over and it's driver, Joel Courtney, got out and bound Wilberger's arms and legs with duct tape. He also covered her body with blankets he had stashed in the back seat. After this, he sped off towards a nearby area that was covered with heavy forestation.

Hours after Brooke was snatched from the apartment complex, her sister Stephanie realized that she hadn't seen or heard from her in a while. She decided to track her down to make sure she was okay, and began with the place she had last seen her—the complex's parking lot. When she got there she was surprised to see an almost empty parking lot, save for the cleaning supplies Brooke had been using and Brookes flip flop sandals, one of which was now broken.

Stephanie immediately ran inside and called police, who immediately launched a missing person's case despite their protocol stating they should wait 24-hours first. Brooke's broken flip flops at her last known location triggered enough of an alarm.

When detectives arrived at the Oak Park apartments, they quickly discovered that her truck, purse, phone, and wallet were all still at the apartments. If she had left the apartments by herself, she had done so without any identification, money, and shoes. It seemed unlikely that this would have been the case.

The search for Brooke began in the same way most crimes do—with the victim's significant other. In this case, Brooke's long-term boyfriend was quickly eliminated because he was over 4000 miles away doing missionary work in Venezuela. Brooke's family was also quickly ruled out.

During this process, the word of Brooke's disappearance quickly got out to the community, and a massive volunteer search was launched by the Wilberger's Mormon church. Within days of Brooke's disappearance, both Eugene and Corvallis were covered in missing posters detailing Brooke's physical appearance and last known location. Over 4000 acres of heavily-wooded area outside of Corvallis was searched for any signs of the missing girl over eleven days. None were found.

Police soon began to realize that the best chance they had of finding Wilberger would be to find the person who had taken her from the Oak Park apartments, so they quickly began to focus on the few early leads they had in the case.

The method in which Wilberger was abducted led police to believe that her abductor was a repeat offender. It's difficult to grab a grown woman off of the streets without anyone seeing or hearing anything. Police began looking through sex offender registries and crime logs to create a suspect pool, one that turned out to include over one thousand names, all of whom were interviewed.

One of the first people contacted by police was 45-year-old ex-con Lauren Hugo Krueger. He had been convicted in 1985 for attempted rape and had served time for the felony assault and kidnapping of a 23-year-old jogger. Krueger had also been questioned in relation to several reports of harassment and stalking. Most damningly, Krueger had also been spotted at a car dealership less than a block away from where Wilberger was abducted from. It was a promising start to the investigation.

Chapter 4

Many police officers in Corvallis believed they may have identified the man who abducted Brooke Wilberger on May 24, 2004, as being Lauren Krueger. He had committed several similar crimes in the past, making him a likely suspect. However, when he was interviewed, police discovered he had an airtight alibi for that afternoon, and he was eliminated in the case.

Shortly after Krueger was eliminated as a suspect, another man by the name of Sun Koo King was identified as a probably suspect. King was an Oregon State graduate who was unemployed and lived in the area. He had recently had a lot of trouble with the law for breaking and entering into Oregon State dorm rooms and stealing their occupants underwear.

Detectives searched King's home and found a startling collection of women's underwear, used tampons, and pubic hair. King also catalogued where he found each object of his collection, which allowed investigators to see that he had gotten most of the items from dorms at the University and from the laundry room at the Oak Park apartments, the same apartments Brooke Wilberger lived in with her sister.

Police were shocked by what they found at King's home, but what shocked them more was that there seemed to be no sign of Brooke Wilberger anywhere. Further, King passed a polygraph test and seemed to have an airtight alibi. Investigators were again forced to abandon the promising lead.

By October 2004, five months after Brooke's disappearance, police had a third strong suspect—Aeryn Evans. Evans had been arrested the month before for attacking a Oregon State student on campus. Evans' step sister called police after the incident suspecting that he may have been involved in Wilberger's disappearance too, but this was quickly discovered to be impossible by police.

Frustrated by having to eliminate three great suspects in a row, police decided they needed to take a different approach in the hunt for Wilberger's abductor. They decided to focus in on the one piece of evidence they had directly connected to the person who took Brooke—a green Dodge Caravan.

Police suspected that the green van was connected to Brooke's disappearance because of the two earlier reports from Randy and Crystal on the Oregon State campus, as well as from a tip call from a man who identified himself as Brian. Brian told police that he had seen a green van driving around the area Brooke was last seen. The driver was acting suspicious enough that the van had stood out to the man. The three incidents were too bizarre for police not to connect with Brooke's disappearance on the same day.

Both Randy and Crystal were interviewed by police, but neither were able to give a clear description of the van's driver. They had both been too spooked at the time. However, the coach that had intervened in Crystal's encounter with the van had gotten a good look at the van itself and was able to provide police with more details, including the fact that the van had had Minnesota license plates.

While police were now convinced that the van seen on the Oregon State University was the van used in Wilberger's abduction, they still had no idea where to find the van, and no idea who had been driving it. By November, 2004, six months after Brooke's abduction, investigators assigned to the case were still on square one. Little did they know though, that another crime was about to be committed in Albuquerque, New Mexico, and this crime would lead them right to Wilberger's killer.

Chapter 5

On November 29, 2004, a 22-year-old Russian exchange student, who goes by the pseudonym Natalie Kirov, left the daycare she worked at on the University of New Mexico campus for home. Minutes away from her doorstep, a car pulled up next to her and a man jumped out and told her to get into the car. Terrified, she complied.

The man held Kirov captive in his car at knifepoint as he drove off. When they got to a secluded area of a dead end road, the man pulled the car over and began to sexually assault the young woman, forcing her to remove her clothes in the process.

After sexually assaulting the Russian beauty, the man declared that he needed a drug fix, a "pick-me-up," and drove to a shady apartment complex to purchase some crack. He left Kirov in his car, bound up with her own shoelaces. While her captor was inside, Kirov managed to free her hands and unlock the car. She immediately ran into the street, despite being mostly naked, and flagged down a passing car.

Just as Kirov settles into the car she flagged down her captor emerged from the nearby apartment. After seeing how terrified Kirov became, her saviours quickly drove off in the opposite direction and brought her to the police station. She was finally safe.

Police immediately responded to Kirov's report by visiting the apartments her attacker stopped in to buy his drugs. They were able to find a lady willing to admit that a guy named Joel matching Kirov's description had stopped by earlier that night. Further, she knew where Joel lived.

Police immediately proceeded to the address given to them and immediately spotted the red car Kirov described parked in the lot outside. Police had just begun examining the vehicle when they were approached by a man who said he owned the car. Police asked him if his name was Joel, and he immediately responded yes. Police responded in turn by arresting him.

The Joel police now had in custody was Joel Courtney—a 38-year-old mechanic fisherman. Joel lived in Albuquerque with his wife and three children, but his marriage was incredibly unstable. Only a few weeks before this arrest, Courtney's wife had taken out a restraining order on him.

When police dug deeper into Courtney's past, they discovered that he had a long standing drug problem that they were able to trace back to his childhood in Beaverton, Oregon. Courtney had grown up an average, loving family, but his life began deteriorating after he started using drugs at the tender age of 11. By the age of 14, Courtney began repeatedly molesting his sister and cousins, and by the age of 19, he began experimenting with satanism, and was arrested several times for sexual assaults.

Now, many years later, he was back in custody for the sexual assault of Natalie Kirov, but it had been almost 20 years since he had been committed a crime, something Albuquerque detectives were skeptical of. They wondered if he had victimized any other women who crossed his path over the years, so they contacted authorities in Oregon, Courtney's home state, to ask if there were any unsolved crimes that matched Courtney's modis operandi. Almost immediately, Oregon police mentioned the disappearance of Brooke Wilberger six months ago, hoping to finally provide some answers to Wilberger's family and the surrounding communities.

Chapter 6

After having Joel Courtney brought to their attention, the Brooke Wilberger taskforce in Corvallis, Oregon decided to look further into Courtney's past to see if they could connect him to Wilberger's disappearance. They were quickly rewarded for this decision.

Investigators soon found out that Courtney and his wife had only recently moved to Albuquerque, New Mexico. Before that, the couple moved around Oregon frequently looking for cheap accommodations. At the time of Wilberger's disappearance, the couple were living with relatives in Portland, Oregon, an hour's drive away from Corvallis.

Further, investigators found that Courtney had been working for a janitorial company in Corvallis while he lived in Portland. He drove the company's 1997 green Dodge Caravan with Minnesota license plates to and from work each day.

Courtney's van was the exact van police had been trying to track down for the last several months. Armed with this knowledge, police managed to track down the vehicle, which was immediately brought to Portland to be searched for any forensic evidence that may have survived. Specifically, they were looking for any DNA evidence to compare to known samples of Brooke Wilberger and Joel Courtney himself.

While investigators waited for the DNA results to come back from the lab, they looked into Courtney's whereabouts the day Brooke Wilberger disappeared. They discovered that Joel Courtney had actually been expected in court to face a DUI charge that very day.

Police learned that on this day Courtney apparently made a call from Corvallis saying he would be late for his court time, but he never appeared. Police also learned that the next day, a disheveled Courtney had shown up at a family member's house 16-hours away from Corvallis. When asked why he was in such a state, Courtney came up with a story of how he ran into a gang of men in the woods who had captured a young woman and forced him to do terrible things he did not want to do. Amazingly, the family member chalked the unbelievable story to Courtney's chronic drug use, and never asked about it again.

On the one-year anniversary of Brooke Wilberger's disappearance, Corvallis investigators finally received the results of the forensic sweep of the green Dodge Caravan. It was worth the wait.

The evidence recovered from the van conclusively proved that not only had both Brooke Wilberger and Joel Courtney been in the green van, but Joel Courtney had been the person to place Wilberger there, and he likely knew where she was now. The final challenge investigators now had was getting Courtney to reveal this information so they could finally bring Brooke home.

Chapter 7

On August 2, 2005, Joel Courtney, who is preparing to go on trial for the kidnap and sexual assault of Natalie Kirov is served an arrest warrant for the kidnap and presumptive murder of Brooke Wilberger. Weeks later, the Kirov case is brought to trial, and faced with the indisputable evidence against him, Courtney pleaded guilty. He was given a sentence of 18 years in prison.

But Joel Courtney didn't have long to get settled in the New Mexico prison system. In April of 2008, he was extradited to Oregon in order to stand on trial for the charges laid against him in Brooke Wilberger's case.

When the trial began in Spring of 2009, the prosecutors in the case showed the court Joel Courtney's long standing history of sexual assaults against women, which dated back to his late teen years. They also presented a witness that had seen Courtney the night before Wilberger's abduction. This individual stated that they used to work together, and that they had spent the night of May 23, 2004, drinking and smoking crack together.

Although prosecutors had a large amount of evidence against Courtney, they were missing something very important, something desired not only by them but also by Wilberger's family and the entire community of Corvallis and Eugene—Brooke.

Up to this point, investigators had been unable to find any indication of Brooke's final resting place, and Courtney wasn't about to give this information up easily. The Wilberger family was all but begging the prosecutors and investigators working on Brooke's case to make a deal with Courtney so they could bring their daughter home and give her a peaceful burial.

The District Attorney eventually succumbed to the Wilbergers' wishes and presented a plea deal to Joel Courtney. The terms of the plea deal stated that Courtney needed to plead guilty to all charges against him and reveal the location of Brooke's remains. In exchange, Courtney would receive life in prison without parole.

Courtney rejected this initial offer, but quickly returned to the bargaining table. Courtney offered to plead guilty to the crime if he could be locked up in New Mexico near his family instead of in

Oregon. He also promised to reveal the location of Brooke Wilberger's remains. Courtney's counter-offer was accepted and signed.

To uphold his side of the plea deal, Joel Courtney drew a map to Brooke's burial site for investigators and walked them through the events of May 24, 2004. He told investigators the story of how he forced the young woman into his van and took her to some nearby woods to sexually assault her. After being raped, Wilberger became enraged, and tried to fight her way to freedom. Courtney responded by punching Wilberger until she fell unconscious before beating her to her certain death with a piece of wood he found nearby.

Based on this confession, and armed with Courtney's map, investigators drove 10 miles outside of Corvallis to a heavily wooded area known as the Coast Range. Their goal: to locate Brooke's remains.

After several days of searching, investigators were finally able to locate Brooke Wilberger's remains in a shallow grave next to a clearing of trees. Her grave was hidden beneath a mound of tree branches and leaves. For the Wilbergers, the news was bittersweet. They finally knew what happened to their daughter, and they finally could bring her home, but up until this point they had always maintained hope that when she came home she would still be alive.

Joel Courtney was formally sentenced to life in prison without parole two months later, and was brought back to a New Mexico prison where he prepared to spend the rest of his days. It was the end of a violent sexual predator's freedom, but most importantly, it was the end of the mystery that had plagued Oregon police and Brooke Wilberger's friends and family for years.

Brooke was finally home and at peace, and the world was a little safer now with Joel Courtney now behind bars. This is little solace to those who continue to miss Brooke Wilberger dearly, but having some answers is inarguably better than none. Those who knew Brooke in life remember her as the sweet, caring angel she was. She had a good soul in her heart and a good head on her shoulders and would have undoubtedly achieved great things in life.

Brooke's family still keep in contact with the investigators that dedicated their time to bringing Brooke home—they attend the officers' retirement parties and exchange the occasional email—a small token of the gratitude they will always hold.

THE MURDER OF CAROL TAGGART

OLIVIA WATSON

On Boxing Day of 2014, a young man living in Fife, Scotland walks into the local police station to inquire about his missing mother, Carol Taggart. The young man is her son, Ross. Carol Taggart has been missing for three days. Her family is desperately worried, apart from Ross, who is still going out clubbing and hitting the town using Carol's credit cards.

Then police find Carol's body, devastating her daughter Lorraine and partner Shaun.

Growing up, the Taggart family were incredibly close. The family comprised of four members, Carol, the mom, Shaun, the dad, and Ross and Lorraine, who were brother and sister.

Ross is four years older than Lorraine and had a different father, but that never mattered to them. The two were very close as children, and Ross always looked out for his sister. Both were loved and cared for by Shaun and Carol.

Lorraine, who was both Shaun and Carol's biological child, was very close with her father. She was a daddy's girl. Likewise, Ross was a momma's boy, and proud of it. Ross and Carol shared a very close relationship, but Shaun always considered Ross to be his son through and through, and to Ross, Shaun was always dad. The two shared many happy father-son memories. Shaun had taught Ross how to ride a bike when he was younger; he had been there to take the training wheels off. They were a typical family of four.

Carol and her son shared a special closeness. Although there was always enough love for Lorraine, there was no denying that Ross had always been the favorite when it came to Carol. There was always a little bit extra love for Ross.

In his mother's eyes, Ross could do no wrong. To her, he couldn't lie, he couldn't cheat. Her family described her as believing that the sun simply shone out of Ross's backside. He was the golden boy.

But in his teenage years, Ross went through some significant changes. As a child, he'd always been a loving, supportive brother and son. He was outgoing, loved to meet new people, and always seemed to be smiling. When he got older, he became very introverted.

As a young adult, Ross never said much. He wasn't a man of many words. When he was displeased, he wouldn't speak up. He would just give an unmistakable look, and his friends and family would instantly know.

For his family especially, this was frustrating. They couldn't get into his psyche, or figure out what he was thinking. They would ask him why he behaved certain ways, but they would never get clear answers from him. Most of the time, they wouldn't get answers at all. Ross would simply give them a blank stare and go to hide in his room, isolated from the family and the rest of the world.

Ross knew he didn't need to work hard to be loved by his family though. He knew he was the perfect child in his mother's eyes, he'd always known it, since the day he was born. The pair had had years together to bond before Shaun and Lorraine entered their lives. They had a mutual feeling that it had always been just the two of them.

Ross was well aware of this connection, and he used it to his advantage. He used his mother's affection against her often, emotionally manipulating her to get his way. To those around Ross and Carol, Ross's behavior showed him to be lazy, unfair, and rude. He was a user and a narcissist. But to Carol, he was none of these things. He needed her, he was her only son, and he relied on her for everything. Ross eloquently played on every emotion Carol had.

Ross was lazy in life and expected everything to land in his lap. He was brought up in a beautiful house, went on beautiful holidays, and had beautiful cars. He was used to getting everything he wanted, so he saw no point in trying to work for anything. That seemed to be his outlook on life—why try when you know it will be provided anyways.

Ross's laziness wasn't a product of his upbringing. Lorraine, Ross's sister, grew up with all the same luxuries as him, but as an adult, she worked hard to make her parents proud. She understood the privileges she had and used them to better her life and become independent. Ross was the opposite.

In the eyes of her father, Lorraine was a roaring success. She worked hard in school, achieved high grades, held down jobs, and went off to college to study dancing, which had been a lifelong passion for her. While this was happening, Ross was at home cruising through life, spending most of it alone in his room or with Carol.

Carol always saw the best in Ross. She saw Ross's laziness as a struggle. She worked hard to please him, to make him know that he was her priority. Ross knew this. He knew he could use those feelings to make his mom support him financially. More than that though, Ross understood that he could play up his role as the helpless son to draw Carol away from other people who saw him differently, especially their family.

Carol defended Ross to no end when others tried to make Carol see she was being taken advantage of, but that wasn't enough for Ross. He wanted to isolate her. He wanted to be her entire world so the money and affection would never stop.

Carol and Shaun had very different ideas of how to deal with Ross behavior as he aged. Shaun wanted to be hard on their son. He believed that Ross, who was now in his early 20's, was old enough to learn how to hold down a job and stand on his own two feet. He thought coddling Ross was holding him back from being an independent adult, but Carol wouldn't hear it. She believed that it would just take time for Ross to come out of his slump. He would grow into a responsible adult; he just wasn't ready yet.

Shaun and Carol began constantly arguing about what to do with Ross. He had begun driving a massive wedge in between his parents. For years the couple argued, unable to come to any resemblance of an agreement on how to deal with their overgrown child. While Shaun was still adamant that Ross needed to become more independent, Carol began to aggressively prioritize her son above all else, even going as far as telling Shaun that Ross came before everything, including Shaun.

After 19 years together, Shaun and Carol separated. It was becoming clear to both of them that they were no longer on the same page in life, and there was no end to their fighting in sight. Both Shaun and Lorraine blamed Ross entirely for the separation.

Shaun was heartbroken by the separation, but there didn't seem to be anything he could do. He couldn't sit back and watch the woman he loved get taken advantage of by her son, especially when he was expected to submit to Ross's wishes as well. Reluctantly, he decided to move out of the family's house.

Now, the Taggart household consisted of Carol, Ross, and Lorraine. While Lorraine was saddened by the departure of her father, Ross was elated. He loved being the man of the house. Lorraine was disturbed by the new dynamic that was developing at home and left as soon as she could. She later described the two years where it was just the three of them together as the longest two years of her life.

After her separation from Shaun, Carol began suffering from bouts of depression, so much so that she was unable to disguise her sadness from her children. In her vulnerable state, Carol was even less prepared to stand up against Ross, who began exploiting her even more.

It was around this time that Lorraine began to understand the kind of person her older brother had developed into. He wasn't a lazy boy with no ambition; he was a user. He was bleeding his mother dry. Lorraine tried to warn her mom that Ross was taking advantage of her, but par for the course, she wouldn't listen. Lorraine was terrified that Ross was going to turn against Carol one day and that Carol would be left with nothing.

Lorraine tried to get her mother help for her depression. The more depressed Carol got, the more dependent on Ross she became, and Lorraine could recognize that that was a recipe for disaster. She went to appointment after appointment with Carol and tried to get her enlisted in different facilities. But this didn't help, Carol's depression got progressively worse. She was lost.

Lorraine recalls feeling incredibly frustrated with her brother during this time. While she was doing everything she could to try and help her mom, he continued to prey on her weaknesses. And for whatever reason, Carol continued to rely on Ross more and more, ignoring Lorraine's pleas and attempts to get her help. Lorraine couldn't crack through the glass that separated herself from Ross and Carol's relationship. As hard as she tried, she was always on the outside looking in.

After years of this, Lorraine couldn't take it anymore. She relented to the fact that Ross was always going to come first in his mother's eyes, and that there was little she could do about this. All she could do was try to make her mother proud by succeeding in her own life, and it was time for Lorraine to focus on this. She couldn't keep fighting a losing battle, so she left home.

Finally, Ross had his mother all to himself. Although at this point in his life, Ross was in his mid-twenties, he had no serious relationships outside of his relationship with his mother. He had cycled through a series of girlfriends, but unsurprisingly, none of them stuck around for long.

Carol, in her depressed state, also had a hard time maintaining relationships outside of Ross. She had no interest in dating, as she still had a strong love for Shaun, and she had little motivation to make or maintain friendships.

Carol and Ross's relationship developed into a non-sexual partnership. The two began going on holidays alone together, and they began spending all their social time together, it was the kind of relationship you would expect to see between a husband and a wife—not a mother and a son.

The more time the pair spent together, the more fused their lives became. Carol was now fully dependant on her son emotionally, but

Ross was still only using his mother to make gains for his own life, and Carol was completely unable to see this for herself.

Although the family of four had been close when Lorraine and Ross were younger, there was now a clear divide. While Ross and Carol were perfectly happy in their closeness, both Lorraine and Shaun found it incredibly strange. And they were no longer alone. Many friends and family members of Carol began questioning Ross's motives. There were very few people outside of Carol that saw Ross as a good man. To most, he was a bad apple.

When Ross recognized that his mother had become fully dependent on him, he began to exert dominant control over her. He no longer felt the need to be sneaky in his manipulations; he was comfortable being outright aggressive with Carol. When she disagreed with Ross or said no to him, he would get angry and withdraw, knowing she would work hard to get back in his good books, giving him everything he had asked for initially and more.

Lorraine saw the shift in her brother's attitude towards their mom and grew increasingly concerned. He was becoming nasty. His tone when he argued with Carol was sharp, condescending, and cruel. It sent the message that he was going to get his way no matter what.

Even though Shaun had been driven out of the family home by Ross, he continued to see Carol. The pair began to grow closer again, and Shaun worked to pry Carol away from Ross just a little bit. For a while, it looked like it was working. Shaun and Carol had grown very close again, and Shaun asked to move back in, thinking they had finally found a way to mend their broken relationship. But things did not go as planned. Before Shaun could move back in, Carol told him that she'd have to ask Ross for permission.

This set Shaun off. Throughout their separation, Shaun had continued to help Carol financially support herself and their children, as her depression had been making it difficult for Carol to work consistently. Shaun helped pay the bills; Ross did not. And Shaun and

Carol were adults. He saw no reason why Ross had any say in the matter. Shaun never moved back into the family home.

On August 11, 2012, Lorraine married her husband on a beautiful sunny day. It was the happiest day of her life, and one of the last happy day the whole family would ever spend together. Shaun proudly walked Lorraine down the aisle, and Carol, elated to be the mother of such a beautiful bride, was too swept up in the magic of the moment to care about Ross's dislike of her re-budding relationship with Shaun. The family was able to celebrate together openly. After this day though, Ross began to isolate his mother from the rest of the family further, something they all thought was impossible. When Lorraine had her first child a year later, Carol wasn't allowed to visit and see her first grandchild for over six months.

In October of 2014, Carol took Ross on vacation to New York City for his thirtieth birthday. Most people at the age of thirty have moved out of their parents' home, have started a career, and possibly even a family. But Ross's life couldn't have been more of the opposite, and he was pleased as punch about that. After they returned from their trip, Carol continued to indulge her son, spending over £1,500 on Christmas presents to give to him before the day even arrived. Unbeknownst to her at the time, Carol would never see Christmas that year.

Out of the blue, on December 23, 2014, Ross Taggart called the Fife police to report Carol missing. He told the operator on the other end of the line that he had gotten into an argument with his mom and she had simply walked out of the house. Because she had been suffering from bouts of depression for years now, he was worried that she had taken the argument too much to heart and had gone and done something terrible.

Investigators charged with looking into Carol's disappearance had several concerns about the nature of this phone call. While Ross sounded confident on the phone, he didn't sound worried.

Additionally, he had made a point of getting information across that isn't common when people usually report family members as missing. He seemed to be trying to set up a specific scenario; it was suggestive and manipulative. Unfortunately for Ross, manipulating the police was not as easy as manipulating his mother. Investigators were wary of Ross from the moment he picked up the phone.

Lorraine had not spoken to Ross in a very long time when she got a missed call from him while out shopping with her husband. She was nervous about why he was calling, so her husband called him back on her behalf. That's when Ross told them the news—Carol was missing.

Initially, Lorraine wasn't too worried. She was hopeful that Carol had merely begun to see Ross for who he was and needed to take some space from him and therefore wasn't answering his calls. She figured she would call her mom later, and Carol would see that it was Lorraine and she would answer. By the end of the day, Lorraine had called her mother over ten times but had received no answer. That's when she began to feel an overwhelming sense of dread.

Lorraine thought of several possible scenarios of why Carol had run off and wasn't answering her calls, and they all seemed to revolve around Carol's relationship with Ross. The most likely, she thought, was that Ross had hit Carol, and Carol had gone into hiding to protect him. Despite how little she liked her brother, Lorraine still never expected the truth to be what it was.

In the days after he reported his mother missing, Ross was closely watched by the police. His movements and actions were caught on CCTV cameras and were being monitored. In the late hours of Christmas Eve, he was seen walking around the caravan park where his mother owned a holiday caravan. A few hours later he was seen withdrawing cash using his mother's card. Even later that same night, he was seen buying drinks at a nightclub, again on his mother's dime.

After Christmas Eve came and went without a word from Carol, Lorraine began to heavily doubt her brother's account of what had happened right before their mother went missing. On Christmas Day, she got a call from the police. They had found Carol's car with her purse, wallet, and phone inside. At that point, they knew something terrible had happened. They knew she was gone.

On December 26, three days after reporting his mother missing, Ross went into the local police station to check in on how the investigation was going. The visit was captured on camera and showed the true lack of emotion Ross was exhibiting during this time. This visit raised further red flags regarding Ross's involvement in Carol's disappearance. There was no recognition of sadness in Ross as he eagerly asked questions about what the police had found out so far. He wanted to know exactly what the police knew, which made them feel like he was trying to figure out something more specific—were they on to him.

Ross's actions after his mother disappeared were suspicious to everyone around him. While his sister Lorraine and father Shaun were at home crying their eyes out, calling people, and trying to wrap their brains around what was happening, Shaun was carrying out his life seemingly as normal. He continued to go out to clubs and use his mother's cards on a regular basis, even buying movie tickets to see *The Hunger Games* at the cinema. He sold Carol's expensive jewelry, justifying the act by saying he was entitled to her estate according to her will. He was not acting as if he'd just lost the person who meant everything to him just a week ago.

By January 1, 2015, Ross was the sole target of the investigation into Carol Taggart's disappearance. The rest of Carol's family had picked up on this, as he had quickly become a topic of interest when police questioned them. Initially, it was just about Ross's behavior in the days following Carol's disappearance, questions like why is he still going out clubbing? Does he have permission to use Carol's cards?

But as time passed, investigators got less subtle with their questions. Eventually, they got to the meat of their queries and asked

Lorraine and Shaun the same question separately: do you think Ross would do something to Carol? Their answer was the same—absolutely.

On January 11, 2015, the Taggart family received the news they had all been dreading: Carol's body had been found.

Carol's body was found stashed beneath a caravan in the same park as Carol's. It was the same place Ross had been seen on CCTV footage stalking around on Christmas Eve. Her body told a horrifying story to police, a story of brutal violence at the hands of someone with nothing but hate in their hearts. She had been battered to death and throttled. Her neck had been broken, and she was covered in bruises. The damage was so horrific that when Lorraine was brought in to identify the body, she was only shown her mother's wrist, which had a distinctive tattoo on it, although decomposition hadn't yet made her face unrecognizable.

To both police and the rest of the Taggart family, Ross was the prime suspect. Above all else, Lorraine was angered that even in death, Ross discarded their mother. She was left outside alone, where it was cold and wet. He didn't make a mistake. He did not feel guilty. He had left the only person in the world who loved him outside in the cold alone for over two weeks, and he didn't seem the least bit sorry.

Three days after police found Carol's body, Ross was formally arrested and charged with his mother's murder. Lorraine and Shaun felt relief for the first time in weeks when they heard the news. It was unfair to them that Ross was allowed to live freely after taking the life of their loved one. They hoped that at least they could now get some answers from Ross on how he was able to commit such a terrible act.

As well as being charged with murder, Ross was also charged with perverting the course of justice after lying to police and taking measures to prevent investigators from discovering what had happened to his mother.

During his trial, which took place in Edinburgh in November 2015, the severity of Ross's attack on his mother became clear to Shaun and Lorraine for the first time. He had beaten his mother with his fists so severely that he had partially broken her neck. He then strangled her so violently that her neck snapped the rest of the way. It wasn't a crime committed from a distance. It wasn't cold and calculated. It had been done with his own bare hands, face-to-face with the woman who raised him, while she screamed out in pain and fought for her life. It was a lengthy, sustained attack, after which he wrapped her body in a sheet, put her in the trunk of her own car, and drove her out to her caravan where she stayed for several days before he went back and buried her beneath a neighboring caravan.

The case against Ross was overwhelming. Everything pointed towards him. The prosecution had been able to assemble hours of suspicious activities captured by CCTV cameras along with 188 witnesses and experts. Including Ross, the defense only presented two.

Just when the family thought they had heard the worst though, the prosecution presented a surprise witness whose purpose was to demonstrate further the lack of remorse Ross had for what he had done.

The witness was a young woman, who neither Lorraine nor Shaun had ever seen before. They soon heard that she had been contacted by Ross through the online dating app Plenty of Fish the night that he had murdered Carol. He was using the app to look for casual sex just hours after dumping his mother's body, unbeknownst to the young woman. To prove that the young woman was telling the truth, prosecutors presented the GPS log from Carol's vehicle. Both the locations of Carol's caravan and the young woman's house appeared on the log in succession.

As well as condemning Ross beyond a reasonable doubt, this information also provided insight into Ross's mindset the night he killed his mother. He was not remorseful in the least. He had felt powerful, dominant, and wanted to continue the adrenaline high he got from committing murder. He wasn't a normal human being—he was a psychopathic narcissist.

Despite the overwhelming amount of evidence against him, Ross took the stand in his own defense and denied having anything to do with the disappearance or murder of his mother. He stuck to the story he told police over the phone when he first reported her missing—she had simply stormed off into the night after an argument. His family, watching from the court, recognized the blank look on his face he always wore when he lied.

The jury in the case took less than an hour to reach a unanimous verdict of guilty on all charges. Ross received a life sentence, which meant he would spend a minimum of 18 years in jail. To Lorraine and Shaun, this was barely justice. He was set to be released from prison at a younger age than Carol had been when she died.

Carol's memory lives on in the hearts of Shaun and Lorraine, but their hearts will be forever broken. Carol had so much love in her, and it was incredibly difficult to see her taken away from them by the person that she loved the most. Ross had been her golden boy, she had given him everything she had and more, and just as those around her feared, Ross took everything from Carol. He took her money, her love, and ultimately, her life.

THE MURDER OF DOMINIQUE DUNNE

ERICA THOMAS

Destined for stardom

In November 1959, film producer Dominick Dunne and actress Ellen (Lenny) Dunne welcomed a new baby to their growing family. Dominique Dunne was the couple's youngest of three children, and their only daughter. Dunne and her older brothers grew up surrounded by the arts – in addition to the influence of their parents, who were active in the California film industry, the children were frequently surrounded by celebrities of the 50s and 60s – close family friends who were often guests at the family home.

Dunne and her siblings grew up in a large house in Beverly Hills, but moved around fairly frequently as Dunne attended schools across the country – in Los Angeles, Connecticut, and Colorado. However, Dunne's childhood wasn't entirely carefree – when she was just eleven years old, Dunne's parents divorced. A few years later, in 1975, her mother was diagnosed with multiple sclerosis.

Still, Dunne pursued her education. After her graduation in 1977, Dunne studied art and Italian in Florence, at the Michelangelo School and at the British Institute. When she returned to California, she worked briefly as a receptionist and translator for Los Angeles' Italian Trade Commission before venturing back to Ft. Collins to study acting at the Colorado State University.

Her studies in Colorado were short-lived, however, and Dunne left after only one year to start auditioning back in California. Just a few weeks later, she was offered her very first film role. Dunne's acting career took off quite quickly – in her first three years, Dunne appeared as a guest on many well-known television shows, including *Family*, *CHiPs*, and *Fame*. And after taking on roles in four made-for-TV movies, Dunne made her cinematic debut as Dana Freeling in the movie "Poltergeist."

"One day, she decided to become an actress and the next week she was on a back lot making a movie, and that from then on she never stopped," said Dunne's father Dominick in a piece he wrote for Vanity

Fair in March 1984. "She loved being an actress and was passionate about her career."

"At ease in a sophisticated world."

To her friends and family, Dunne was known as a friendly, kind person. Despite having grown up with wealth and fame, Dunne's father described her as "totally at ease in a sophisticated world without being sophisticated herself." Indeed, Dunne dressed in casual clothes, preferring jeans and t-shirts to the upscale fashions her peers sported – and drove a blue Volkswagen Bug convertible.

Dunne loved cooking, traveling, baseball, and languages – particularly Italian, which she continued to speak quite fluently. She also loved animals, and had a soft spot for unwanted strays. Dunne adopted a cat with a lobotomy, a large dog with stunted legs, a snake, and a rabbit, among many other cats and dogs.

Even before her role in "Poltergeist," Dunne was a firm believer in supernatural phenomena, and friends say she was strictly superstitious.

Instant attraction

Dunne met John Thomas Sweeney in 1981, when she was twenty-two and he was twenty-five. Sweeney worked as a chef at Los Angeles' trendy "Ma Maison" restaurant, and Dunne was immediately drawn to him. After their initial introduction at a party that autumn, the pair quickly fell into a romantic relationship – and moved in together only a few weeks later, into a rental house in West-Hollywood.

However, their passion soon resulted in the first of many quarrels between the couple. Dunne was, by that point, well-known in Hollywood – a popular girl with many friends. Sweeney, on the other hand, had grown up poor in Pennsylvania, the product of a troubled family life. Despite Dunne's attempts to include him in her world, Sweeney felt like an outsider and was ashamed of his uncultured family history.

While Dunne had grown up with a loving family that respected and addressed emotional issues, Sweeney was raised in a coal town with an alcoholic father who, his mother claimed, often dealt with his frustrations by beating her – often in front of their children. By the time he was fourteen years old, his parents had divorced, and his father had developed epilepsy.

"Bitterly ashamed of his family and filled with a sense of worthlessness because he was a member of it, (Sweeney) longed to escape into a larger and more exciting life," read an article published in *People* magazine in 1983.

Sweeney's desire for a better life led him to pursue a culinary arts diploma from a local community college. At the age of twenty, he crossed the country to California, where he landed a job working at a restaurant called "Picolo's." Only one year later, he started as a chef's apprentice at "Ma Maison."

He was a talented, ambitious chef – and was willing to put in the work to achieve his career goals. After two years of double shifts, Sweeney was given a leave of absence to spend a year working on the French Riviera before returning to "Ma Maison" – where he worked as chef Wolfgang Puck's chief assistant.

His position at the glamorous restaurant gave him an opportunity to get a first-hand look at the elegant world he so desperately wanted to be a part of. And, after meeting Dunne, he finally felt like he would be able to access it. However, along with his excitement at being with a talented Hollywood actress, there was fear and insecurity – and the lasting sense of worthlessness he felt as a result of his troubled family life.

His jealousy started to take hold of the relationship. His interactions with Dunne grew more patronizing and dominating, and he began showing up on sets where Dunne was working to intimidate her male colleagues. Eventually, even that wasn't enough – Sweeney started to come to Dunne's rehearsals and even her acting classes.

It seemed Dunne couldn't do anything on her own without having to first discuss it with her boyfriend, which usually resulted in an argument that Dunne would never win. The more Dunne resisted Sweeney's possessiveness and jealousy, the more frightened he would be that she would ultimately reject him. Often, this fear would become anger.

"Alex said he was scary."

Dunne had introduced Sweeney to her family during the summer of 1982, flying the two of them out to New York where most of her family lived. According Dominick's article in Vanity Fair, Dunne's brother Alex was the only one who had "voiced his dislike" of her new boyfriend.

"Although I could see that Sweeney was excessively devoted to her, there was something off-putting about him," Dominick said.

The first night, Alex told his father about an incident that had happened after Dominick had left the restaurant. Dunne had been recognized by a man in the bar, who called out her iconic line from the film "Poltergeist." According to Alex, "there was no flirtation," just an excited, if slightly tipsy, fan.

"When Sweeney returned to the table and saw the man talking to (Dunne), he became enraged. He picked up the man and shook him," stated Dominick. "Alex said that Sweeney's reaction was out of all proportion to the incident going on. Alex said he was scary."

The next day, Dominick was to meet Dunne and Sweeney for lunch. Although he said he arrived at the restaurant late, the couple still wasn't there – and Dominick was already on his second bottle of Perrier by the time his daughter showed up with her boyfriend.

"I was immediately aware that she had been crying, and that there was tension between them," Dominick said. "The lunch was not a success. I found Sweeney ill at ease, nervous, difficult to talk to. It occurred to me that (Dunne) might have difficulty extricating herself from such a person, but I did not pursue the thought."

Getting physical

As the couple began fighting more and more, Sweeney's reactions frequently turned violent. On August 27, 1982, Sweeney reportedly tore out handfuls of Dunne's hair after grabbing it and using it to knock her head repeatedly against the floor. Dunne managed to get away from Sweeney and fled to her mother Lenny's house, with Sweeney following close behind. While Dunne's mother refused him entry and even threatened to call the police, it was only a few days before Dunne forgave her boyfriend and returned to their home.

Despite Dunne's forgiveness, Sweeney attacked her again not even a month later. On September 26, during another argument, Sweeney grabbed Dunne by the neck and pushed her to the floor before he started to choke her. Luckily, a friend heard the loud gagging noises coming from the next room – "it was the worst sound I had ever heard" – and came in to break up the fight.

"He tried to kill me!" Dunne cried out. Sweeney denied her accusation, insisting that Dunne come back to bed. Instead, she went into the bathroom, where she escaped out a window to spend the night with a friend.

The next day, Dunne showed up at the set of *Hill Street Blues*, where she was to guest star as an abuse victim for an episode of the show. According to accounts from cast and crew on the set, the bruises on Dunne's face and neck were "realistic" enough that she hardly needed any make-up for her role.

Dunne spent the following days in hiding, trying to avoid the abusive, angry boyfriend who was searching for her. Eventually, she contacted him to end the relationship – and to demand he leave the home they rented together so she could live there alone. Still, knowing how unpredictably angry and violent Sweeney could be, Dunne changed the locks of the house before moving back in without him.

The final battle

That autumn, Dunne had taken on a new role – playing Robin Maxwell for the three-episode science fiction miniseries *V*. She'd

completed filming the scenes for the first episode and was nearly
finished with the second episode on October 30, when she invited her
co-star David Packer to rehearse scenes together at her home.

The pair were hard at work when Sweeney called Dunne at around
8:30 p.m. – and then showed up at the house only ten minutes later.
Dunne answered the door with the chain fastened, but Sweeney
demanded she come out and speak with him. Packer asked if he should
leave, sensing Dunne's discomfort with the situation, but she said she
wanted him to stay while she stepped outside to deal with her
ex-boyfriend.

Out on the driveway, an argument broke out. Sweeney was
pleading with Dunne to forgive him and take him back, but Dunne
refused. She'd reached her limit and was no longer willing to tolerate
Sweeney's anger and violence. Like he'd done before, Sweeney suddenly
reached out and grabbed her firmly by the neck, dragging her up along
the driveway into the next-door neighbour's back yard.

Dunne was no match for Sweeney – the petite actress was a mere
5'1" and 112 pounds. Sweeney, 6'1" and close to 200 pounds, held her
down and began to strangle her. She was unable to fight him off, and
eventually fell unconscious.

Meanwhile, Packer watched the confrontation with growing fear
– he could see Sweeney's obvious rage and jealousy. When he heard
screams followed by a thud, he called the police, only to be informed
that the location was outside of the department's jurisdiction. After
hanging up with the officer, Packer called a friend and left a message
on his answering machine explaining that if he was found dead, John
Sweeney should be held responsible.

Eventually, Packer went outside to check on Dunne, and found her
lying on the driveway with Sweeney crouched next to her. Sweeney
asked Dunne to call the police, and this time, they said they would send
an officer. When the police arrived and found Dunne still unconscious,
they called an ambulance, which arrived only five minutes later.

Brain-dead

On the way to the nearby Cedars Sinai Hospital, Dunne's heart came to a full stop, but doctors were able to restart it once the ambulance arrived. However, examinations showed that Dunne had sustained extensive damage from the anoxaemia during her strangulation – and that although her heart had been restarted, there was no way for doctors to reverse the death of her brain.

"There were tubes in her everywhere, and the life-support system caused her to breathe in and out with a grotesque jerking movement that seemed a parody of life," Dominick recalled. "Her eyes were open, massively enlarged, staring lifelessly up at the ceiling. Her beautiful hair had been shaved off. A large bolt had been screwed into her skull to relieve the pressure on her brain. Her neck was purpled and swollen; vividly visible on it were the marks of the massive hands of the man who had strangled her.

It was nearly impossible to look at her, but also impossible to look away."

The hospital's staff did everything they could for Dunne, and after five days, her parents made the decision to remove her from the life-support systems that were keeping her alive. Dunne died instantly, and her heart and kidneys were donated to the hospital to be used for transplants.

Dunne's tragic death was a shock to the entire Hollywood community, particularly for Dunne's extensive network of family and friends. Hundreds of people attended Dunne's funeral, held on November 6 at the catholic Church of the Good Shepherd in Beverly Hills – the same church where Dunne had been baptized 22 years earlier. Her body was laid to rest near Los Angeles, at the Westwood Memorial Park.

"An act of passion and despair."

"If (Dunne) had been killed in an automobile accident, horrible as that would have been, at least it would have been over and mourning could have begun," Dominick said. "A murder is an ongoing event until the day of the sentencing, and mourning has to be postponed."

Sweeney was charged with Dunne's murder, and the case finally went to trial at the court in Santa Monica in early August, 1983. A *People* magazine article from October 1983 described Sweeney as a "young man in a black suit" seated at a long table, his face "white as an egg" and his large, pale hands "folded meekly" over a Bible.

"It is the fashion among the criminal fraternity to find God, and Sweeney, the killer, was no exception," Dominick remembered. "The Bible was a prop; Sweeney never read it, he just rested his folded hands on it. He also wept regularly. One day, the court had to be recessed because he claimed the other prisoners had been harassing before he entered, and he needed time to cry in private.

"I could not believe that the jurors would buy such a performance."

But Sweeney painted a very different picture in the courtroom than the true colors he'd shown to Dunne's family and friends. According to Sweeney's testimony, Dunne "provoked" the violent struggle that resulted in her death, because she had previously agreed to reconcile and had then refused to take Sweeney back. Sweeney said he "just exploded and lunged toward her" after she told him she'd been lying when she said she would live with him again.

He added that he "had no memory" of the event, only that he found himself next to Dunne's unconscious body, with his hands pressed around her neck. According to Sweeney, he tried to resuscitate her, and when that didn't work, he ran into the house and swallowed two bottles of pills – attempting suicide due to his panic and regret at what he had done.

Sweeney's lawyer Michael Adelson added that Dunne was a "snob," who was constantly telling Sweeney how he was beneath her. Sweeney's account of their relationship presented Dunne as two-faced and heartless, and he said she even told him that she had been leading him on.

Dominick even recalled receiving a phone call from the prosecutor for the case, district attorney Steven Barshop, in July, shortly before the trial was set to begin. Barshop explained that Adelson had requested that Lenny not be allowed in the courtroom – Adelson felt the presence of the victim's mother, confined to a wheelchair, would create "undue sympathy for her that would be prejudicial to Sweeney."

The "accident" was a "tragedy," Adelson argued, "not a real crime – an action of passion and despair."

However, no evidence could be found to back up Sweeney's story, and investigators were reluctant to believe him. There was nothing to support Sweeney's claim that he'd attempted to commit suicide, and even during his initial interrogation, Sweeney seemed to show little remorse for his part in Dunne's death.

In fact, the police officers who arrested him testified that Sweeney had seemed "quite calm and collected," and more concerned about what would happen to him than what had happened to Dunne – only about an hour and a half after he'd been arrested.

"I fucked up, I can't believe I did something that will put me behind bars forever," Sweeney reportedly told police when he was brought down to the station. "Man, I blew it. I killed her. I didn't think I choked her that hard. I just kept on choking her. I just lost my temper and blew it again."

When one of the officers made a comment about how well Dunne had been doing with her acting career, Sweeney retorted, "well, I was doing quite well in *my* career. I'm quite proud of what I've done."

Upon further investigation, it was revealed that Sweeney had obviously strangled Dunne for about five minutes – at least four minutes, according to the medical examiner. According to police, this makes Sweeney's story fairly improbable. Not only would Sweeney have had enough time to realize what he was doing while he was choking his ex-girlfriend, he would have had the opportunity to regain control and let Dunne live.

During the trial, Dominick remembers Barshop holding up a hand to the jury, silencing the room for a four-minute period – "how long it took for Dominique Dunne to die," Barshop said, in his opening statement.

"It was horrifying," Dominick said. "I had never allowed myself to think how long she had struggled in his hands, thrashing for life. A gunshot or a knife stab is over in an instant; strangulation is an eternity."

Barshop also brought forward testimony from one of Sweeney's previous girlfriends – a secretary named Lillian Pierce, who'd also lived with Sweeney. During their relationship, which lasted from 1977 to 1980, he'd abused her on at least ten different occasions – resulting in two separate hospital visits, one for a perforated eardrum and collapsed lung, and a second time with a broken nose.

"Later, we heard that (Pierce) had sat in a car outside the church at (Dunne's) funeral and cried," Dominick said, "feeling too guilty to go inside."

The testimony proved that unlike what Sweeney's lawyer had argued, this was not a unique crime of passion, but rather a pattern of abusive behaviour toward women. Still, Sweeney's lawyer was able to convince the judge that the testimony was prejudicial, and had it excluded from the trial.

"Her account of her relationship with John Sweeney was so shocking that it should have put to rest forever the defense stand that the strangulation death of Dominique Dunne at the hands of John Sweeney was an isolated incident," wrote Dominick. "He was, it became perfectly apparent, a classic abuser of women – and his weapon was his hands."

As he questioned Pierce, without the jury present, Adelson inquired about a specific discussion the witness had had with himself and another lawyer on November 3, 1982 – the day before Dunne was officially removed from life-support and pronounced legally dead.

"Even while (Dunne) lay dying, efforts were being made to free her killer by men who knew very well that this was not his first display of violence," Dominick said. "I felt hatred for Michael Adelson. His object was to win; nothing else mattered."

Testimonies from Dunne's friends and co-workers were also ruled out after Sweeney's lawyer argued that they were nothing but hearsay. These statements explained that Dunne was not remotely interested in a reconciliation with Sweeney – in fact, she'd spent the final five weeks of her life in "permanent fear" of her abusive ex-boyfriend.

Even without this important evidence, the prosecution still sought a second-degree murder conviction, with a minimum sentence of fifteen years.

The jury did get to hear a letter found by Dunne's friends, addressed to Sweeney but obviously never sent to him. The letter detailed Dunne's frustrations at the control Sweeney attempted to hold over her, and her desire to end the relationship.

"You do not love me. You are obsessed with me. The person you think you love is not me at all. It is someone you have made up in your head," Dunne said in her letter. "I'm the person who makes you angry, who you fight with sometimes. I think we only fight when images of me fade away and you are faced with the real me.

"The whole thing has made me realize how scared I am of you, and I don't mean just physically. I'm afraid of the next time you are going to have another mood swing. When we are good, we are great. But when we are bad, we are horrendous. The bad outweighs the good."

An unsatisfying result

The trial wrapped up at the end of September, and the jury found Sweeney guilty of voluntary manslaughter – to the shock of Dunne's family and friends. "The law protected him," the jury said, but several members later admitted that had they known about Sweeney's history of violence and abuse, they would have found him guilty of the second-degree murder charge.

"I guess there is never any real satisfaction that the legal system can give, but this – the outcome – was such a blow, such a slap in the face to our family and to (Dunne's) memory," said Dunne's older brother Griffin. "They literally got away with murder... the bitterness of that will never leave."

Even Superior Court Judge Burton S. Katz, who presided over the trial, felt the system failed to provide justice for Dunne's tragic murder. Barshop stated that this failure has allowed a "time bomb" to return to the streets, where he could potentially abuse again, and blames Katz for the many rulings he made that prohibited the jury from hearing important, relevant evidence.

However, Katz argued that he had no choice but to rule the way he had – but admitted that some of the more controversial rulings during the trial "pained" him. Shortly after Sweeney's trial, Katz moved to the Juvenile Court in Sylmar.

"Nothing is more difficult than rendering a decision based upon a law with which you disagree," Katz said. "Unfortunately, following the letter of the law sometimes doesn't permit one to pursue the ultimate goal of justice."

Sweeney ended up with a sentence of only six and a half years in prison, the maximum sentence imposed for convictions of voluntary manslaughter. Instead of the fifteen years the prosecution had hoped for, Sweeney was released from a medium-security state prison after spending three years, seven months, and twenty-seven days in custody.

"Three and a half years for a life is certainly not justice," Katz said. "If I could have given him 25 (years), I would have given him 25. If I could have given him life, I would have given him life... I agree with everyone that based on his past record of violence... he is dangerous to any woman."

Soon after his release from prison, Sweeney found another high-paying job as a head chef at a chic restaurant in Santa Monica called "The Chronicle." The new position didn't last long, though -

Sweeney was fired after Dunne's family and friends descended on the restaurant with handbills that were distributed to guests and passers-by.

"The hands that prepared your food strangled Dominique Dunne on October 30, 1982," the handbills read.

Sweeney left Los Angeles for Seattle in 1989, and changed his name to John Maura. According to some sources, he is currently employed there as an executive chef for a chain restaurant.

"This guy gets to be reinstated as the head chef in a restaurant as if nothing ever happened," said Dunne's older brother, actor Griffin Dunne. "If she had lived, she'd be an actress everyone in the world would know... he's a murderer; he's murdered and I think he will do it again."

Another friend of the family echoed these thoughts, adding that "the verdict almost says it's okay to kill the one you love."

THE MURDER OF FAITH HEDGEPETH

JESSI DAVIS

Happy-go-lucky

In 1982, Connie Hedgepeth had her hands full with two teenage daughters and a husband who was addicted to drugs. Her marriage was struggling when she took a pregnancy test, hoping the result would be negative. It wasn't. Her youngest daughter was born eight months later, and Connie named her Faith.

"I felt like it was my faith in God that helped me through that situation," she said. "My faith helped me to continue to work and to do what I needed to do for my children."

Still, Connie divorced her husband when Faith was still young. Struggling to stay afloat, Connie turned to her oldest daughter, Rolanda, for support. Despite an almost 18-year age difference, Rolanda and Faith developed a strong bond – "part mother-daughter, part sister," Rolanda explained.

"We were always close. I was kind of like a second mom, but there was that sister bond, too," she said.

Rolanda's daughter Alexis was born on Faith's first birthday, and the two girls grew up together in rural North Carolina. Her upbringing was difficult, but Faith's positive attitude and eagerness to contribute propelled her through her schooling. She was an honor student, a cheerleader, and a regular volunteer for many other clubs and organizations.

"She always had this energy about her," Rolanda recalled. "She was really happy-go-lucky."

Faith's father had dropped out of college to raise his family, and Faith intended to pick up where her dad had left off. She earned a Gates Millennium Scholarship to the University of North Carolina at Chapel Hill – the very school her father had been attending. Poised to be the very first college graduate in her family, Faith had plans to become a pediatrician or a teacher once she completed her education.

Instead, the Native American biology major never made it to her 20th birthday. Police records reveal that Faith was last seen alive at approximately 3 a.m. on September 7, 2012, when she and her roommate Karena Rosario came home after an evening partying at a local nightclub.

The Thrill of a lifetime

The night before she was murdered, Faith had been studying with Karena at the Davis Library, on the university campus. At around 8 or 8:30 p.m., Faith took a break from her studies to send a text to her father – "Hey Daddy, I love you," the message read. She also texted her niece, reminding her to register to vote in the upcoming election.

At around midnight, the girls left the library and stopped back at their apartment before heading out at approximately 1 a.m. to arrive at a nightclub called The Thrill.

Just after 2:30 a.m., the girls left the bar. Karena was feeling sick after having had too much to drink, and wanted to go home. Faith helped Karena get into bed, and then fell asleep herself. However, a text message from Faith's phone was received at 3:40 a.m. by Brandon Edwards, Karena's ex-boyfriend.

"Hey b. can you come over here please," the message read. "Karena needs you more aha. You know. Please let her know you care."

A few minutes later, another text comes through that simply says, "than." It is suspected that the message was intended to fix a typo in the original message, correcting it to say "Karena needs you more *than* you know." Brandon didn't reply until the next day, when Faith's phone received a text at 4:16 p.m. that read, "Who is this?"

At around 4:30 a.m., Karena left the apartment to go over to a friend's house – and claims that she did see Faith asleep at that time. When she returned at around 11 a.m., however, she found her roommate's body in her room, in her bed, "covered by a blanket on top of her slightly askew mattress with large amounts of blood."

At 11:01 a.m., a 911 call came from the house.

Faith was unconscious and cold, Karena told the dispatcher who took the call, and there was "blood everywhere." She said she thought there may have been an altercation, explaining to the dispatcher that "there were items in the room that were not hers and that it looked like someone else had been there."

Police responded immediately, securing the scene at the girls' apartment complex and collecting evidence. They found Faith's body "positioned on the floor, leaning against the bed, with her shirt pulled up and no clothes from the waist down."

Medical examiners concluded that the cause of death was blunt force trauma, based on the severe beating Faith had endured. When the autopsy report was unsealed nearly two years after the killing, it was revealed that she also had bruises and cuts all over her arms and legs, as well as blood underneath her fingernails.

"It's very, very hard, learning of how Faith died," said Rolanda. "She was beaten, she was bludgeoned to death. A lot of people don't understand what that means, but it was really bad."

A rape kit had also been performed, indicating the presence of semen – with DNA that matched other DNA that police had recovered at the scene. Law enforcement officials have not confirmed whether the sexual activity was consensual or forced.

Searching for suspects

In the years since Faith's death, multiple search warrants have been executed – as well as numerous court orders for things like cell phones, computers, and even social media accounts. DNA testing has also been carried out on many of men that interacted with Karena and Faith while they were at the nightclub, but so far, investigators have found no matching results.

While at The Thrill, Faith was reportedly dancing with a man named David Bell. He told police he didn't know Faith very well, and was not named by police as a suspect during the investigation.

"(Redacted) was identified as walking out of Club Thrill with Faith Hedgepeth shortly before the homicide occurred," read a police report unsealed in 2014. "He was the last male to be seen with her before her death."

The report added that Bell admitted to talking with Faith the night she was killed, and to meeting her the weekend before. He refused to provide investigators with a sample of his DNA, claiming that he had likely touched her at some point during the night of the homicide. His statements to law enforcement officers were also determined to be "inconsistent" with statements provided by others.

Another man, Jacob Beatley, was interviewed by police and also not named as a suspect. Karena visited him during the early morning hours of September 7, after leaving the apartment she shared with Faith. DNA was also sought from a man named Reginald Leonard Jackson II, who was not named as a suspect despite having been texting regularly with Faith in the days prior to her murder.

However, none of this information was offered to Faith's family until the documents were unsealed in 2014.

"All they have said to us and to the public, to the media, to everybody, (is) that this wasn't random – how do they know that?" said Chad Hedgepeth, Faith's brother. "Do they have a suspect? Do they have any suspects? ... Tell us something, because being in the dark on any and everything these past four weeks has been brutal."

While the recording from the 911 call seems to indicate that Karena was alone when she discovered Faith's body in their apartment, the police report stated that she returned to their home with a friend. In the recording, however, Karena consistently claims "I just walked into my apartment," instead of saying "we." There is also no sound recorded that could be attributed to another person in the room.

An analysis of the call could suggest that the repetition of the statement "I just walked into my apartment" is an attempt to establish an alibi – especially since the recording reveals that Karena says this several times before even providing the dispatcher with necessary information like the victim's state or the location of the emergency.

At no point in the call does Karena specifically ask for help for the victim. She also apologizes to the dispatcher, using language that analysts typically see in calls where guilty knowledge is indicated.

Initially, law enforcement turned their attention to Eriq Takoy Jones – an ex-boyfriend of Karena's who lived in the same apartment complex and was reportedly an aspiring rapper. Just a few months before the murder, Karena had filed a restraining order against Eriq, on the basis of domestic assault. Police had previously investigated claims that Eriq had kicked two of the doors in the girls' apartment completely off their frames, and eyewitness accounts reported that Karena had been seen with visible injuries to her body – inflicted, she said, by her ex-boyfriend.

"Faith took Karena to take out a restraining order," said Faith's father, Roland Hedgepeth. "I think that very possibly, Takoy may have had some ill feelings toward Faith for doing that."

Rolanda said Faith had moved in with Karena after the restraining order had been filed, to help her friend as she recovered from the abusive relationship.

"I wasn't worried about Faith at the time," Rolanda said. "I wanted them to be safe. I just wanted both of them to be safe."

Just before Faith was murdered, Eriq posted a chilling message on his Facebook page, and texted a similar message to an acquaintance.

"Deal Lord," the post read. "Forgive me for all of my sins and the sins I may commit today. Protect me from the girls who don't deserve me and the ones who wish me dead today."

An unnamed person who claimed to be a former roommate of Faith's called the Chapel Hill Police Department the day after Faith's body was discovered with additional concerning information about Eriq. According to the caller, Faith had told her that Karena's boyfriend hated her (Faith) and told her that if Karena wouldn't get back together with him, he would kill Faith.

However, Eriq was very cooperative with law enforcement during the investigation into Faith's murder. Both his apartment and car were combed for trace evidence, and his DNA was tested and cleared.

"From what I knew of her (Faith), she was the sweetest person in the world. If you needed her and she could do it, she was there," Eriq told news reporters after Faith's murder. "I'll be honest with you – whoever did this deserves to burn."

Investigators also learned that the ex-boyfriend of Karena's that Faith had texted in the hours before she was killed had also been present that night at The Thrill. Police records indicated that Brandon Edwards had even spent the night at the girls' apartment the night before the murder – making his response to Faith's texts the day she was killed quite unusual.

According to a friend named Marisol Rangel, Karena and Brandon were "just friends" at the time of Faith's murder. Marisol is the friend who was reportedly with Karena when she discovered Faith's body, but the 911 operator was confident that Karena was alone when the call was placed.

In January 2013, police released a profile of the killer. According to the profile, developed by Chapel Hill Police and the FBI's Behavioral Analysis Unit, the person responsible for Faith's murder might have been familiar with her – and possibly even lived near her in the past.

The individual may have also "made comments" about Faith in the past, with their behavior shifting after the murder occurred. Obviously, the profile indicated this person would have been "unaccounted for" during the early morning hours of September 7, 2012. Police also stated the DNA evidence collected at the scene of the homicide points toward a "male suspect."

At the time, Faith's father Roland said the development of the profile marked a "new beginning" in the investigation, and believed it would help police solve the case.

"For us, we're kind of stuck back on September 7," he said. "Every day, we get up and relive that day. But I'm confident things will open up soon."

Strange evidence

Nearly two years after the murder, police released a shocking and mysterious piece of evidence. A spiteful, handwritten note was found scrawled on a fast food bag left near the crime scene, with the words "I'M NOT STUPID BITCH JEALOUS."

Police believe the note was written by the killer, but have not said whether the handwriting has ever been officially analyzed. According to private investigator and forensic handwriting examiner Peggy Walla, some clues can be determined from the note.

"What struck me was how clean the document is – the crime scene was pretty bloody, and there's nothing on this document," she said. "Looking at it, I would get the impression it was either written outside of the crime scene, or it was written before, like a premeditation."

She also feels the words were written by a non-dominant hand, indicating that whoever wrote the note was attempting to "disguise" their penmanship. The block letters could be taken as the writer's attempt to distance themselves from authority, she said.

"The word and sentence phrase 'I'm not stupid' is a hot push-button factor," Walla added. "That's probably the most important thing said. This was a jealous person who was called 'stupid.' The person that said it who is now deceased has no way of repeating this person is stupid, which is another way to shut them up."

Users of online forums have also speculated that the use of the word 'jealous' could indicate that the writer of the note was a woman, as the word is thought to be more frequently used by females. The formation of the letter 'P' in particular has also struck some as seeming feminine in nature.

Other speculation surrounds the intent of the note. The words 'jealous' and 'bitch' suggest that the note was not meant for the police of for the public – rather, these deeply personal words were likely intended toward Faith, or possibly even Karena, who would eventually find the body. But more curious yet is the situation that must have occurred that led to the writing of the note. What happened before Faith was murdered?

Cries for help

A clue may be found in a voicemail left for a friend the night of her death. The call appears to have been a pocket-dial – a very timely pocket-dial that potentially recorded the final minutes of Faith's life. The timestamp on the nearly unintelligible message indicates that the call was made while Faith was still at The Thrill, but some have argued that a glitch in technology could have resulted in an incorrect time.

According to President and CEO of Creative Forensic Services Arlo West, who is certified by the New York Institute of Forensic Audio in enhancement, authentication, and analysis of both audio and video, the names 'Rosie' and 'Eriq' appear throughout the recording – potentially referring to Karena Rosario and her ex-boyfriend Eriq Takoy Jones.

"I've worked on hundreds, if not thousands, of cases where people have pocket-dialed somebody," West said. "If you can peel back those layers of noise, you start to get a better picture of the dialogue that is contained – stuff that starts to make a little more sense."

In his analysis for Crime Watch Daily, West identified two distinct female voices – one which he claimed is Faith Hedgepeth, and the other he describes as a "very angry female." He also picked out at least two male voices.

"I hear what I believe is Miss Hedgepeth's cries for help," West said. "You can hear her emotive voice, the tone of her voice, is clearly in pain ... You can clearly hear what I believe is Faith pleading. She's being hurt, being attacked."

West said he feels "very confident" about hearing the names 'Rosie' and 'Eriq,' and included both names in his transcript of the three-minute recording.

He also claims iPhones were "inherently problematic with timestamping" during the time Faith was killed – which he said accounts for the timestamp on the voicemail showing 1:23 a.m., while police believe Faith was killed sometime after 4:30 a.m. Still, Chapel Hill police did contact West for an official analysis of the recording.

"If it is Faith being murdered, and captured in this recording – which I think it is, this is pivotal," West said. "It should be able to solve this case."

Police seem to believe that the voicemail was recorded from the club, not from the apartment – and in the middle of the call, there appears to be music playing or someone rapping. There is also no evidence to support that the name 'Rosie' could have referred to Karena, and Eriq Takoy Jones was apparently called 'Takoy' by his friends.

Still, the voicemail is difficult to discount – especially since, on the night Faith was murdered, it appears to have recorded an emotionally-charged, angry discussion. To many listeners, including members of Faith's family, the voices sound agitated – belligerent, fast-speaking – and seem to be punctuated by audible yelps of what could be pain.

"From day one, I heard my daughter screaming in the background," said Faith's father, Roland. "I knew something was going on."

"A really good case."

The note, the voicemail audio, and other documents – including the 15-page autopsy – were unsealed in September 2014. According to Chris Blue, Chapel Hill Police Chief, the effort was an attempt to generate new leads in the investigation.

"We have excellent evidence – we have a really good case," he said. "We just need to connect this really good case with the killer."

However, in those two years, police had been unable to connect any potential suspect with the crime. The official documents were sealed during that time despite repeated requests from lawyers and news organizations to open them to the public, as investigators felt releasing the information would compromise their efforts.

"It's not that it might hinder this investigation, it will hinder this investigation," said Durham County Assistant District Attorney Charlene Franks.

She added that details contained within the documents, including the 911 call where the crime scene and body are vividly described, could help police identify the killer – as that information would have been known by very few people.

In a "cold case," Franks said, police will often turn to the public for assistance. However, since the investigation into Faith's murder is ongoing, solving the case means keeping the public – including Faith's family – in the dark about some vital details.

"The most important thing to them and the state and the Chapel Hill Police Department is to find the killer of their baby girl, Faith Hedgepeth," she said. "The only way to do that is to keep those items sealed because the information contained in there, other than (investigators), only the killer knows."

According to Steve Hale, private investigator and retired homicide detective who was never involved with the case, it's typical for law enforcement to keep the details of a case under wraps – interviews and tips that haven't been influenced by media reports can make or break a case.

"If there is a suspect, he may not know he's a suspect, and they're waiting for him to get careless and maybe make a comment to an accessory after the fact," he said, adding that detectives likely suspected someone who knew Faith and might have had a distinct motive.

Each document pertaining to the case was reviewed by Judge Howard Manning before being unsealed in 2014. Still, three investigators with the Chapel Hill Police Department and State Bureau of Investigation continued working exclusively on the unsolved case – and offered a reward of $40,000 for any information leading to the arrest and conviction of Faith's killer.

"We really want to bring some peace to Faith's family," said Blue. "This has been two unimaginable years for them."

"Your imagination starts to run wild."

Connie was contacted three hours after Faith's body was found, by a crisis counselor who told her little more than that her 19-year-old daughter Faith had been found dead in her apartment – the victim of what appeared to be a violent homicide.

"I said, 'you must have the wrong girl,'" Connie remembers. "She told me it was her, and I said, 'I don't think so.'"

It fell on Connie to contact the rest of the family, spreading the devastating news to her son, her ex-husband, and her eldest daughter, Rolanda. At that point, Connie said, she didn't have much to tell them other than that Faith was dead.

"They couldn't tell us very much because they didn't want to jeopardize the investigation," she explained. "Not knowing anything at all... your imagination starts to run wild."

Even after detectives brought the family to Chapel Hill, about 80 miles away from their home in Hollister, Connie still had no answers to her many questions. She wasn't even permitted to visit the crime scene, or see her youngest daughter.

"I just wanted to hold her hand, to let her know I was there," Connie recalled. "I still cry for my baby, and I wonder if she called out for help. Did she cry for me? These are the things you think."

Finally, the family was told the cause of death – but without any kind of motive or indication of what could have happened to lead up to Faith's murder, the new information was difficult for the family to process.

"It is getting harder, not knowing what happened, trying to accept what happened," said Rolanda. "She was beautiful. She didn't deserve it. She had a lot going for her."

While no arrests have been made, and no suspects even identified, Chapel Hill Police Lt. Josh Mecimore said police are still confident that the killer will be found and brought to justice.

"Someone knows something, and we're continually appealing to the public to come forward," he said. "This is not a cold case. We are still following up on things, still pounding the pavement, still waiting for that one piece of evidence that will help us solve this case."

Connie, Rolanda, and the rest of the Hedgepeth family are clinging to the same hope.

"At some point, God will let us know what happened," Rolanda said. "Even when I'm down, I still believe that we will find that person."

However, neighbours remain concerned as a result of the limited information available – and the fact that police have yet to make an arrest. While law enforcement officers continued to reassure nearby residents that the incident was an isolated event, neighbours wanted more answers.

"It's not a reassuring thought to wonder if you can send your kids to safety to the bus stop or if something could happen," said Anna Salomon, who lived with her husband and children in the subdivision next to the apartment complex where Faith was murdered. In the weeks following the killing, the neighbours banded together to walk children to the bus stop in collective groups.

Keeping Faith alive

One year after Faith was killed, students at the University of North Carolina gathered on campus at the Bell Tower Amphitheatre for a silent walk in celebration of the student's life. She was also made an honorary member of the Alpha Pi Omega Sorority, the country's oldest Native American Greek letter organization.

"She was the happiest person I knew, always laughing, always smiling," said Faith's friend Leslie Locklear.

Another friend, Victoria Chavis, remembered Faith's "bubbly personality."

"She had a smile that was just infectious," she said, "and she was a wonderful person to be around."

"The entire Carolina community grieves for the loss of this promising, vibrant student," added UNC Chancellor Carol Folt.

The family has honored Faith's memory by establishing the "Faith's Smile Scholarship" in her name – an award which will go to Native American women entering their freshman year of college. The scholarship project gives the family something positive to focus on while they continue searching for answers.

"It's really hard – hard because of not knowing what happened and not knowing why it happened, who did it," Rolanda added. "One little piece of information could break the case, could give us some type of peace. How could somebody withhold that, after everything we have lost?"

Still, for Connie, nothing can extinguish the shining light that defined her youngest daughter, Faith – no matter how many years go by with the case remaining unsolved.

"We don't want anyone to forget her smile. She was a beautiful girl, she was my baby," Connie said. "Her spirit is right here today."

bonus:

On a seemingly normal Thursday afternoon on the Catawba River in May of 2008, two jet skiers planned on having a picnic together along the river when they stumbled upon a peculiar sight that would change their lives forever - a car crashed into a stump on the banks of the river along with the horrifying sight of a dead body lying next to it. They quickly alerted authorities and soon discovered that the body was that of a deceased young woman.

This was the tragic fate of Irina "Ira" Yarmolenko, a University of North Carolina college student who had just celebrated her twentieth birthday several days earlier. She was discovered with three items from her car tied around her neck. There was no sign of a struggle or any clear indication of a motive. She was not sexually assaulted or robbed.

Although first responders initially thought her death could have been a suicide, her death was ruled a homicide by asphyxiation. To this day, her murder still garners interest from the public due to the strange yet disturbing circumstances surrounding her death. Add to that the whispers that surround the case about the possibility that her convicted murderer, Mark Carver, might actually be an innocent man. What followed this horrific discovery was an investigation into the crime scene and into her personal life to uncover what happened to Ira.

Ira's early life and college experience

Ira Yarmolenko was born in the Ukraine on May 2nd, 1988 but emigrated to the United States when she was eight, along with her parents and brother Pavel. The family reportedly fled the Ukraine as refugees due to religious persecution. Her parents, both research scientists, were able to find job opportunities in North Carolina.

Ira quickly picked up the language and by all accounts seemed to assimilate well into American culture. She lived in North Carolina for most of her life, spoke with a southern accent and had several personal interests. Like most teenagers, she enjoyed hiking, acting, photography, sports, and music.

She also played the piano and liked listening to bands, such as the Counting Crows. She was also extremely academic. She excelled in math and science while being an active member of her high school poetry team. Ira was especially close to her family. Although she left Chapel Hill for UNC Charlotte, about a 3-hour drive away, she spoke to her mother almost every day. After her death, her mother said to reporters, "I don't think what I'm living is called life anymore."

During her two years in college, she found other interests beyond her required coursework at UNC Charlotte, where she was an undeclared major but had a strong interest in French. She was a photographer for the University Times, her college paper, and occasionally wrote columns and articles for the Niner Online, an online student-run newspaper.

She was also a member of the university's Russian Club as Russian was her first language. Her Russian language classmate described her as, "the kind of girl that always made you feel special, wanted, needed, cared for, and loved. It always seemed like she was always so happy to see you, and would always take at least a second of her time to say hello to you." It was here that she met her roommate Masha, another student from the Ukraine.

Masha and Ira bonded over the fact that they both spoke Russian and came from similar backgrounds. Masha described the day that she found out Ira was murdered when two investigators showed up at the small apartment that she shared with Ira, "It was her student I.D. picture. And I just started screaming. Sorry. Both of our families immigrated here to this country for a better life and sacrificed so much." Like most people close to Ira, Masha was devastated to hear the news of her friend's death.

Most people who knew Ira described her as outgoing. They felt that she would not have been afraid if a stranger had approached her. She was involved on campus and worked at a local coffee shop, Jackson's Java. Years after her death, her picture could still be found on the counter of Jackson's Java. She had a lasting impact on those that knew her. Her brother said, "Everything that she's ever done was to help people."

At UNC Charlotte, she had many close friends and acquaintances who described her as a cheerful and bubbly person, yet still high-achieving. In addition to her job at the coffee shop, Ira also worked as an aid in a computer lab on campus. The week before finals, her roommate Masha and friends threw a party for her 20th birthday.

During this party, her friends reported that Ira ended up cooking for everyone there, despite the fact that party was a celebration in her honor. This was not uncommon for her to do and was just the kind of person she was. Her friends concluded the celebration by visiting an art exhibit. They reported that she was in good spirits and that they parted amicably.

Although it seemed Ira was thriving in her environment at UNC Charlotte, she was in the process of closing her chapter there and beginning a new one at UNC-Chapel Hill, a school a bit closer to home. "Ira indicated she was sad to leave her friends behind at UNCC, but she was looking forward to attending UNC-Chapel Hill in the fall," according to Sgt. Tindall, an investigator in the case.

She had resigned from her positions at the coffee shop and in the computer lab where she had worked during her sophomore year shortly before she was murdered. Her brother Pavel, a then Ph.D. graduate student at Duke said, "She was not sure how she felt about leaving Charlotte. But she was very, very excited about coming to Chapel Hill."

Ira intended on transferring to UNC-Chapel Hill to be closer to her family and to major in public health. The day of her murder, she visited the coffee shop and said goodbye to her friends there and left a gift, a book, for her former boss. She also took several items to the Goodwill to donate and visited her credit union where she deposited some checks before heading to the river about 20 miles away.

The scene of the crime

The Catawba River is over 200 miles long and spans two states. It is located about 20 minutes from Charlotte and is popular among fisherman, boaters and jet skiers. First responders on that fateful day described a perplexing, yet disturbing scene.

The doors on the driver's side of Ira's car were opened, and her body was found just a few feet away. It did not appear she was sexually assaulted or robbed, nor did she have defensive wounds from fighting off her attacker or attackers.

Three ligatures were found around her neck: a nylon ribbon from a bag in her car, a drawstring from the hood of a jacket and a bungee cord. The drawstring was wrapped around her neck. The ribbon was wrapped once around her neck and oddly tied in a bow in the front. Her hair and body were also wet, although she was found on dry ground.

According to Detective Terry during the trial, "Her head was back towards the embankment. Her feet were near the river underneath some brush. Upon closer inspection, she was actually holding some of that brush in her hand. . . ." It was determined that this was the place where she was murdered and that she had not been transferred there.

Investigators began piecing together her movements before arriving at the river banks and determined it was likely that she headed down to the river banks to take pictures, as she was an avid photographer. Her brother Pavel said he "wasn't surprised she would go to such a remote spot. She was adventurous. She once hiked the Stampede Trail in Alaska with friends, searching for an abandoned bus made famous by Jon Krakauer's book Into the Wild."

Her camera was found in the trunk of her car, but there was not any film in it that could yield any clues about her death. Investigators quickly began interviewing people along the river to see if anyone had heard or seen anything out of the ordinary and came across two fishermen who were fishing about 100 yards from where Ira's body and car were discovered.

Mark Carver and Neil Cassada were cousins who grew up in the area and had been fishing in a new spot they had discovered the weekend before. This spot was about 100 yards from where Ira's car and body were discovered. Carver had been excited about the spot. He had returned to it because it did not require him to haul his boat to the river which was difficult for Carver to do since he suffers from carpal tunnel syndrome, a condition that makes his hands extremely weak.

His doctors recommended he not lift anything heavier than five pounds. Cassada also suffered from a heart condition, making it difficult to do anything too physical. Investigators questioned both men who reported that they had not seen Ira or had not heard anything from their fishing spot. They did report hearing a scraping sound that sounded like noise from construction.

They both willingly provided their DNA to investigators and went on their way. With the lack of forensic clues pointing toward any viable suspects, it was not until forensic analysis of the car several months later revealed partial DNA matches for Carver and Cassada that they became the prime suspects for Ira's murder. Mark Carver and Neal Cassada were arrested in December of 2008, seven months after her death and charged with conspiracy and murder. A day before Cassada's the trial began in 2010, Cassada died of a heart attack. Carver has always proclaimed their innocence.

"Simple" life of Mark Carver

Simple is the word often used to describe Mark Carver. "Simple in his routine, simple in his thought process, simple in his desires and wants," defense attorney Brent Ratchford said to reporters. Unlike Ira, Carver is not well-educated and has limitations with writing and reading comprehension, which he has struggled with throughout most of his life.

At an early age, he was placed in special education classes because of these limitations and his relatively low IQ. At 16, he dropped out of school to work in a mill. At the time he was arrested, it was documented that he was taking medication prescribed for schizophrenia.

Carver is also the father of four children from two different marriages. "He lived for his children and family," his sister-in-law Robin Carver said when asked about him. "He didn't really do much of anything else. Fishing and hunting and family, that was about it."

Although his family speaks well of Carver, like most family members often do, he did have prior brushes with the law despite never being convicted of a crime. In 2005, Carver faced a charge of injury to property. Carver purportedly confronted two people he thought were stealing his four-wheeler. The charge was dismissed, and the file no longer exists. A year before Ira's murder, Carver accidentally shot his son. Carver and his son were supposedly wrestling when the gun went off. "It was an accident," his son said. The case was later dismissed and Carver never convicted of a crime.

Cassada also had had his own dealings with the law. In 1995, he was accused of assault and injury to personal property. He reportedly pointed a gun at someone. But the charges were dismissed and the details remain unclear.

His family insists that he had nothing to do with Ira's murder and that the stress of the trial for a crime he did not commit ultimately led to his death. Kaye Cassada, Neal Cassada's wife said "After 37 years of loving that man and being married to that man, I know he is not capable of hurting anybody. He would have died to help somebody." Charges against Cassada were dropped, a common proceeding with deceased suspects. His family attended the hearing and his son Shannon Cassada said, "We want everybody to hear that he was an innocent man."

Carver also maintains his own innocence, stating "they said that they had ... my DNA and Neal's DNA in the car. I know that's a lie because Neal left, and they couldn't have gotten no DNA because I wasn't down there. I didn't go around it. I didn't go around the car. You know what I'm saying?" He also said he didn't think Cassada would commit such a crime because "He's got four young'uns himself."

Although lie detector tests are not reliable enough to be used in court, during the initial investigation Cassada took a polygraph test, which he passed. Because he passed, investigators did not give Carver one. Carver has been very vocal about his willingness to also take a polygraph test.

Touch DNA

During the investigation and trial, Carver never wavered in proclaiming his innocence and said this to Ira's family "I never seen her that day. If I'd knowed she was up there, I would have went up there and helped her. They could have easily come down and killed me just like they did her."

His trial began in 2010. Before the trial, Carver was offered a surprising plea deal from the prosecution: 4-8 years in prison if he pleaded guilty to second degree murder. Had he taken this deal and pled guilty to murder he could be out of prison and with his family. His attorney said, "I have never gotten such a low offer. And to me that spoke volumes about the case." Carver turned down this offer and prosecutors moved forward with the case.

Prosecutors argued that the two men killed Ira because she witnessed or photographed something they did not want her to see. As a result, they strangled her and pushed her car on the embankment where their DNA was transferred to the car. Their intention was to sink the car in the water, but it hit a stump where it stayed until it was finally discovered by the jet skiers. They then returned to their fishing spot until they were questioned by police.

Prosecutors relied on a relatively new forensic technique at the time known as "touch DNA." Unlike previous methods, touch DNA uses smaller amounts of DNA, such as skin cells transferred to a person or object when they come into contact with someone. But touch DNA is not as reliable as other DNA methods requiring blood or saliva because it is difficult to determine the origin of these cells. For instance, skin cells can be transferred indirectly by a third party or carrier.

For example, a man in California was falsely imprisoned because his DNA was found on a murder victim. It was determined that it was impossible that he was a killer because he had a solid alibi. At the time of the murder, he was unconscious in a hospital due to extreme intoxication.

Prosecutors then discovered that the same paramedic who treated him for intoxication was a first responder at the murder scene. The DNA from the intoxicated man was presumably transferred to the victim by the paramedic. This case set a precedent about the reliability of touch DNA and is cited by Carver's advocates for innocence as a possibility as to why Carver's and Cassada's DNA was found on Ira's car.

Despite this interesting theory, it was not presented by the defense in Carver's trial and the jury found him guilty of murder. He was sentenced to and is currently serving life in prison. Carver's advocates argue that the car and crime scene was not preserved, and that Carver and Cassada's DNA could have been transferred by officers or other people near the crime scene. Many officers, the jet skiers, first responders were all present at the crime scene and could have all inadvertently transferred the DNA to the car.

Several other inconsistencies exist in the prosecution's case. Carvers DNA was not found on her body nor on the trunk of the car where he and Cassada would have pushed it into the river bank according to prosecutors. Carvers DNA did not match a third DNA profile found on the bungee cord and the only DNA found under Ira's fingernails was her own.

His attorney and advocates also argue that the two men couldn't have physically pushed the car into the river bank due to Carver's carpal tunnel and Cassada's heart condition. Cassada supposedly got winded just walking. In 2013, Carver's attorneys filed an appeal on his behalf, but the appeals court determined "no error in the defendant's trial" occurred, meaning his conviction of life in prison would be upheld. But this did not deter his advocates from trying to prove Carver did not receive a fair defense during his trial.

Earlier this year, a judge granted the request of the North Carolina Actual Innocence Project, attorneys who have become interested in Carver case who believe Carver is wrongfully imprisoned, to see DNA reports that were never shared with Carvers defense team, along with further DNA testing.

They argue that Carver did not receive a proper defense as his lawyers did not call any witnesses or DNA experts to the stand and address the DNA evidence, and that the DNA evidence is not compelling enough beyond a reasonable doubt to warrant a life sentence for Carver. It is the only evidence linking Carver to the crime. Only time will determine the final outcomes of Carver's appeals as the evidentiary hearing has been postponed. Legal proceedings could take several years.

Other suspects

If Carver and Cassada's DNA was indeed transferred by a third party and they did not kill Ira, then who did? There was no one in her life that seemed to have any motive. Besides these two men, there was only one other suspect in her murder investigation. Nine months after the murder, Christopher Lemont Cooper wrote a letter to News anchor Erica Bryant to "confess a sin," that he and several other accomplices had killed Ira.

He said he drove a van full of friends that were all high and needed money for drugs. He said he was unable to sleep "because of what we did to that young woman." And wished to meet with the reporter. The TV station did not publish the letter and turned it over to investigators where they took the letter very seriously and launched an investigation with the North Carolina State Bureau of Investigations.

Police and investigators visited Cooper, where he was in jail on charges of rape, assault by strangulation, and for being delinquent in child support. He reportedly refused to cooperate with investigators, but they ultimately ruled him out as a suspect concluding that several of the accomplices he named were incarcerated at the time of the murder. They also cleared the other accomplices named in Cooper's letter and continued building their case against Carver and Cassada.

Free Mark Carver

Free Mark Carver is one of the prominent websites advocating for the release of Carver. They believe he is innocent or at the very least did not receive a proper defense in his trial. The website is run by a former newspaper journalist who now works in the fashion industry. She had no ties to the case or families and became intrigued with the case in 2011 after its details aired on Dateline NBC and through other online news articles.

One of the major theories from Carver's advocates presented on the website is that Ira was not murdered and in fact committed suicide by placing the ligatures around her neck herself. They claim that Ira was not the cheerful person described by her friends and loved ones and that she had battled depression.

Her boyfriend had broken up with her shortly before her murder and her poetry was sometimes dark and melancholy. The website alludes to accounts from unnamed people who claim that Ira had attempted suicide when she was younger and had seen a therapist at UNC Charlotte. The website does not provide sources and only mentions them as letters to the author.

Although this theory may be offensive to those who loved Ira and describe her as a happy and vibrant young woman, it has been addressed by pathologists who have dismissed this theory saying "For this to have been anything but a homicide, i.e., this was a suicide, this victim would have to tie three ligatures around her neck tightly and before death get into this position while that's going on and her legs underneath the brush given that position and I just feel like that was not consistent with what we are seeing. . . . Yes, and another thing that this illustrates a little bit better also is the presence of particular matter, soil and grass on her skirt as well. So that's another thing that would have had to happen. If this was a suicide she would have had to do all this stuff by herself. It is just not consistent with that theory."

Her brother Pavel, who has since completed his Ph.D. in biomedical engineering and continues to conduct research at a pediatric hospital, said he has read some of the internet theories about his sister's death, but they are "not grounded in reality." He asserts that his sister never attempted suicide and there was no indication she was depressed. Nevertheless, the fact remains that a lively, young woman lost her life just days after her 20th birthday.

Memorials

We may never know what really happened to Ira or why someone chose to take her life but it is clear that she touched many people who strive to keep her memory alive. The jet skiers who found her body, Dennis Lovelace and Brenda Pierce, placed a memorial cross where they found her car. The changing levels of the Catawba river sometimes covers part of the cross, but it is still visible to visitors.

A memorial bench as far as Alaska, where Ira spent a summer waitressing, also bears her name. "A Kansas City based artist Shane Blindt designed and installed this bench at the request of many co-workers whose lives were touched with Ira's presence during the 2007 McKinley Village Lodge summer season. Lettering on the memorial was hand drawn with pen showing the elegance and beauty of Ira's outward expressions contrasted with a raw and rugged placement into the world she left behind." It is maintained by locals there.

Her high school poetry team in Chapel Hill renamed the group The Sacrificial Poets in her honor.

What Time Devours is a book written by her former professor at UNC Charlotte who dedicated his book to her memory. He directed a campus production, which Ira was a part of the previous year before she was murdered. He also included a line from her poetry and her picture in the dedication of the book.

The controversy around her murder continues to intrigue people and several websites and pages are dedicated to outlining the details of the case. Ira's murder has been featured on Dateline and 20/20. She continues to captivate an almost cult following, and many people are still tirelessly working to prove that Carver is innocent and did not receive a fair trial. If this is the case, it means that justice has not been served for Ira and her family. But one thing is for sure, the memory of Ira Yarmolenko will continue to live on with her family, friends, and strangers that have been touched by her story.